"Jan speaks the liberating language of the bo[...] Yes, I like that a lot! Her truth telling cuts rig[...] nasty schemes. He is such a scoundrel and sp[...] guage of a liar. Jan helps us shake free from the myths that bind and blind us as we embrace life-giving truth."

Patsy Clairmont
Women of Faith
Author of *Stardust on My Pillow*

"When Jan Silvious speaks, I listen. Having had the privilege to work in women's ministry with her in past years, I have found that her heart is attuned to God and to women. She is trustworthy and informed, making her one of the most effective in women's ministries today."

Babbie Mason
Singer, songwriter, and author

"Twenty years ago, Jan Silvious appeared in my life and, by God's design, dusted off a very special place and became a precious friend! Only God knew what a difference it would make for me. Time and again, Jan has challenged my out-of-balance thinking in her no-nonsense manner, led me toward the truth, and then said, 'Sandy, be strong and do hard things!' How I love her for that!

This gifted woman, with her great wisdom and straightforward manner, speaks to myths that, for most of us, at some time in our lives, to some degree, cloud our reasoning. So I encourage you to open these pages with great anticipation for there will be 'ah-ha' moments, 'oh-my' moments, and whoops of joy when you discover that where you are isn't necessarily where you have to stay."

Sandy Smith
Speaker, Conference Coodinator
Bailey Smith Conference Ministries

Moving Beyond The

MYTHS

Hope AND
ENCOURAGEMENT
FOR WOMEN

JAN SILVIOUS

The poem "Take Over," by Ruth Harms Calkin, is from her book, *Tell Me Again, Lord, I Forget* © 1974. Colorado Springs: David C. Cook. All rights reserved.

The meditation "In Those Days" (March 2, 1980), by Deborah Jean Morris Swindoll, is from *The Tale of the Tardy Oxcart,* compiled by Charles R. Swindoll, © 1998. Word Publishing, Nashville, Tennessee. Used by permission. All rights reserved.

All Scripture quotations, unless otherwise indicated, are taken from the *New American Standard Bible®,* © Copyright The Lockman Foundation 1960, 1962, 1963, 1968, 1971, 1972, 1973, 1975, 1977, 1995. Used by permission.

Scripture quotations marked (AMPLIFIED) are taken from *The Amplified Bible* © 1965, 1987 by Zondervan Publishing House. Used by permission.

Library of Congress Cataloging-in-Publication Data

Silvious, Jan, 1944-
  Moving beyond the myths women believe: hope and encouragement for women / by Jan Silvious.
     p. cm.
  Includes bibliographical references.
  ISBN 0-8024-6584-6
  1. Christian women—Religious life. 2. Christian women—conduct of life. I. Title.

BV4527 .S445 2001
248.8'43—dc21

00-051519

1 3 5 7 9 10 8 6 4 2
Printed in the United States of America

To my grandchildren
Lauren, Luke, and Rachel

"I have no greater joy than this,
to hear of my children walking in the truth."
3 John 4

The prayer of my heart for each of you is
that you would know the truth
and the truth would make you free

CONTENTS

FOREWORD

My friend and co-worker, Jan Silvious, is tenaciously passionate about a few things. One of them is the truth. She grabs hold of lies that hold women in bondage, and she won't let go. Jan just isn't satisfied until mythical thinking is replaced with the truth and she sees captives set free.

Jan and I have the unique advantage of being friends for thirty years, and in that time we have shared many ministry opportunities; but one of my most treasured times with Jan is when we meet weekly on Sunday evenings to co-host Precept Live, our national call-in program where we give "God's truth—uncompromising and wrapped in love." We pray, we laugh, we discuss, and sometimes go round and round as we sharpen one another's iron, and then we share the microphone—and it happens. We do the most important thing we can do—we bring God's Word to the table, proclaiming God's truth that sets people free.

I often sit amazed and in awe at my friend's ability to go to the core problem. Jan has a way of getting to the bottom line. She is like a searchlight moving over the dark waters looking for a response to the all-encompassing questions: Where is it written? Where is the truth? Where is the lie? Where is the myth?

Because Jan loves loves the Word of God and steeps herself in its precepts, she is fearless in going into the deepest pits to offer hope and encouragement to people who have missed the truth and as a result suffer the conquences. I learn so much when I listen to Jan. I stand in awe when I see and hear the way our Lord uses her, whether it is from a platform, one-on-one, or over the air. Jan Silvious is a woman who listens, who cares—a female Barnabas, a daughter of encouragement, whose message is deeply needed.

We are seeing unprecedented numbers of women who are dealing with anger, low self-respect, fear, and depression. There are woman who are floundering in a turbulent sea of misery. Jan has expressed to me over and over that her passion is that women would learn to think truth, speak truth, and live truth so that the truth can rescue them and set them free.

That is why it is an honor for me to write the foreword to this much needed book, *Moving Beyond the Myths: Hope and Encouragement for Women.* This is a book you'll want two of—so you might as well buy an extra copy now. Once you begin reading this book, you won't want to let it go—but immediately you'll think of others who must have it, and have it now: women who need to move from destructive myths to life-giving truth.

How I pray that you will take Jan's advice and question everything you read and then listen with that wonderfully probing question: *Where is it written?* Be a woman who is willing to dig out the answer for yourself.

The truth is here . . . it will set you free . . . and this is the book that will put you on the path.

KAY ARTHUR
PRECEPT MINISTRIES
CHATTANOOGA, TENNESSEE
2000

ACKNOWLEDGMENTS

Writing about myths can take you into a world of smoke and mirrors that requires the clarity of good minds and great souls to help stay focused on the truth. God provided those good minds and great souls for me in the form of some women who read the material, reasoned through the myths, and embraced the truth. All of our lives have been richer for the experience.

I want to thank the Arkansas Group. Your diligence and encouragement helped more than you will ever know. Thanks so much for joining in the journey.

My gratitude to the Chattanooga Group. I'm crazy about you all. Each of you is a trophy of God's grace and joy.

How can I say enough about Jo McCarthy, Pam MacRae, and Moody Conference Ministries? You have been unflinching in your support through the years and your vision for the Moving Beyond the Myths seminars has been unbelievably encouraging.

To Lynda Elliott, Anita Lustrea, Carolyn Capp, Claudia Hackney, and Susan Walker. You read these words while they were "cooling" on the page. Your enthusiasm and your "Go, girl!" did not go unnoticed! Thank you, thank you, thank you!

To each of you who cheered me on! We made it! To God be the glory. He loves us and has shown it one more incredible time! What a God we serve.

MISERABLE MYTHS

They are everywhere. They are pervasive, invasive, and all-consuming. They are virtually unrecognizable but do they have power! I am talking about the myths that cause women misery. One myth often leads to another that is tucked a little deeper than the first in the psyches of bright, unsuspecting women. These are women who cannot figure out why their choices lead them to painful dead ends. Like the magician's scarves, their myths are tied one to another; and once they begin to recognize them, it is amazing to see the multicolored myths pour out. You may have a thought that you are questioning; you may be believing a myth.

To uncover the myths is to give yourself a chance to find the truth. To keep protecting your myths leaves you with a "no life," "no power" existence. When you don't know what to believe, what is real, what works, what is safe, you are left in misery. Maybe that is where you see yourself. Maybe misery is your lot and you hate it. I hope that if you are miserable you really do hate it and that you are willing to look at why you are hurting.

I don't know about you, but I am unwilling to live there.

I want all of the life God has given me.

If I suffer, I want it to be with a purpose.

If I am discontent, I want it to work for my growth.

I want all of the power God means for me to have, and I would love to blame someone else when I don't experience life and power. I have walked with God long enough to know there is no one to blame but me when I fail to live in the victory that is already mine. It is my own laziness, cowardice, people-pleasing, and fear that keep me from embracing all that God has for me!

MY PERSONAL MYTH HUNT

I don't believe that God wastes any experience in our lives. It is just up to us to "get it." It is up to you and me to realize that what is going on right in front of our eyes is significant and loaded with lessons if we will just look, listen, and be open. God says that His wisdom is available if we ask (James 1:5). Our problem usually stems from the fact that when we encounter a difficulty, we apply the remedy we assume will work. It is not our habit to ask God right off the bat. We usually have to muddle with the situation for a while. Then, when we do ask God, we don't believe the answer is really from Him. But if we don't "get it," it's not His fault but ours. None of us truly wants to look at reality versus what we *want* to believe.

I had been a Christian for only a couple of years, and yet I was zealous for ministry. I wanted to help people be better because they knew God better. My eyes had been gloriously opened, and I wanted others to experience the same awakening. Through an odd set of circumstances that only God could have orchestrated, I found myself standing by the bed of a woman who had overdosed on prescription drugs. She had talked with me a day or two before, crying that her husband didn't love her. She told me that she had done everything she could do to make him love her, but he never seemed to care the way she wanted. The next thing I knew, I received a call that this dear, deceived soul had tried to kill herself with an overdose of drugs.

When I saw her writhing in that hospital bed, I knew this had not been a fake attempt just to get attention. She had been deadly serious in her effort to stop the pain. If death was what would take away the hurt, then death is what she wanted. She had to have the love of that man—her life was a "living death" anyway. At least that's what she believed. So she tried to just check out. I watched in horror as I leaned over her bed trying to communicate with her. She was gasping for breath and clawing the air, trying to grab hold of an imaginary hand. I couldn't believe that she had really done this, and yet she had. I knew that *what she believed* had driven her to it.

The myth that was bigger than life to her was this: I have to have the love of my husband or my life is not worth living. (Not to leave you hanging—shortly after she recovered, he left her for good. The last time I saw her she was slowly trying to recover her life and find some purpose for living. Her pain was still incredible, but at least her focus was on living instead of dying.) She was my first memorable encounter with a myth-believer—and it was what she believed that nearly killed her.

Of course, there was a point in my own life when I had to recognize that I was hanging on to my own little set of well-protected myths. I came to the Lord as a twenty-six-year-old wife and mother of three. Although I was raised in the church—a very good Bible-teaching church—a relationship with Christ never had "taken" fully with me. I dabbled with a foot in the Christian world, a foot in the secular world, and one finger in an Edgar Cayce book checking out the possibilities of reincarnation. I knew that there was more than I was living. I knew that my beliefs weren't completely true, but I wasn't sure what was. I had a good husband, three handsome sons, a home, two cars in the carport, and a load of misery.

Why couldn't I be happy?

What was wrong with my husband that I couldn't be content with him?

Why weren't my boys enough to satisfy me?

Why did I have such a fear of death, and why did I panic when I thought of leaving this life?

Why did I want to look wherever I could, including the paranormal, for answers? I was so confused.

Finally, God reached out to me, challenged my lip service to a very shallow concept of Him, and called me to Himself. It was at that point that I began to see that there was more to life than I had assumed.

God was working. He was in control, and although I might not understand some of the things I experienced, everything happened with a purpose. There was a whole lot more to life than what I could see, touch, and hear around me. That relationship with Christ started thirty years ago. It has been quite a ride. Every significant turn in the road has come into my life with the exposure of some myth and the embracing of God's truth.

After I began to grow through intensive Bible study, opportunities to talk with women like the dear woman fighting for her life in the hospital began to multiply. Each of these women was stuck at some point in her life because of a myth she had embraced.

- One of the first women I talked with was a woman whose pastor-husband refused to let her wear hairspray, makeup, or any "adornment" because he just didn't like it. She was sad and lonely as she told of all the prohibitions in her world.

- Another whose story has been repeated over and over was a woman who could not believe that God could really forgive her affair. How could God forgive and love a person who would commit such a wanton act?

- There was the woman whose elderly husband died in the hospital while she went home to spend the night. She wasn't with him, and she just couldn't believe that she would ever get over the guilt of it.

- I nearly despaired as I talked on many occasions with a woman who had walked away from her husband and children to live with a lesbian lover. She hated it but believed that she was homosexual and had no other choice.

The list compiled over the years is incredible and innumerable. In fact, I eventually ended up working with a Christian psychologist on a regular basis. There I encountered woman after woman whose life was shattered. Needless to say, I think I have seen a lot, but I can tell you I haven't seen it all because I never cease to be surprised at the myth-twists that present themselves in the desperation of women's questions.

No matter what insanity she may be confronted with, the Christian woman invariably asks, "How can I change what is going on in my life and still be godly?" That's a big one for us. We have bought into the mythical thinking that "questioning is sin." If we buck the system that has us in bondage, it is not godly. If we fail to go along with the status quo and this causes a problem, then we are wrong.

In his book *The Healing Path,* Dan Allender writes, "Until we become discontent with the rigors of trying to escape our powerlessness we will live locked into the present *status quo.* If we are fully at home in our situation, then we will not ponder a better tomorrow. Discontent is the mother of invention. Discontent is holy when it compels us to dream of redemption."[1] Oh, my sisters, would that we "dream of redemption" and dare to examine our discontent with the status quo!

Every time I move forward, I have to tell myself, "I am willing to take responsibility for what I believe because I know it determines how I live!" What about you?

Are you with me?

Are you willing to take the grown-up plunge into examining the beliefs upon which you hang your life?

If so, let's move on.

THREE MYTH CATEGORIES

I have done an informal survey of a limited number of women. They are ethnically diverse, some employed in high-powered executive positions, and others in the most menial of service jobs. Some are married, some are divorced, some have never married, and some are widowed. Some of them work in established ministries, and some are just beginning to walk as followers of Christ. All are involved in mainline churches in the United States. My question of them was, "Tell me the myth that has caused you the most misery." I defined a myth as a belief assumed to be true. When I gathered their responses, it was fascinating to see that the myths mainly fell into three categories: *relationship to God, relationship to self,* and *relationship to men.* I think you might be interested to take a look at what some of them had to say. These are your sisters in Christ, and probably many of them are your sisters in heart. See if you relate to them in any area. Don't be too quick to discount yourself from their thoughts. Remember, there are many myth-scarves tied together, and they all relate in some way.

Here is a random sampling of their myths:

- I could never be happy unless I had a man.

- I had to "find" myself in order to be fulfilled.

- I could be successful by winning awards and getting better jobs.

- Once divorced, always the sinner.

- God will always bring along a special man, but if He doesn't, some-how life won't be what it should have been.

- Opposites attract and make the best mates.

- Two halves make a whole.

- If I am accused, I must be guilty.

- I have to become one with my spouse to the point that I sacrifice myself to the extent of losing my identity and individuality.

- Men are just big boys.

- "Wife" is a synonym for "mother."

- Marry a man who claims to be a Christian and you will have a Christian marriage.

- Save the marriage at all costs (death, loss of identity, ill-treatment, and the destruction of your children).

- I should be happy.

- If my marriage is bad, I should be sad.

- Don't question authority, particularly male authority.

- If you do what is pleasing, your husband will be devoted to you.

- I am responsible for everything, whether it is good or bad.

- I am wrong.

- My needs are secondary to everyone else's needs.

- Your husband will earn a living for the family.

- Women work outside the home because they are ambitious for more, and they don't put their families first.

- You aren't a family if you are divorced.

- I can't live without intimacy (sex and nurturing).

- I must have a romantic connection to heal from my past.

- God is good, but He is not enough for my problems.

- God has one plan for Christian women. If you do something different, you are probably stepping outside the will of God.

- If your husband has an affair, it is your fault. You did not give him enough sex or good food.

- God expects a lot out of me. If I live up to His expectations, He will treat me well. If not, then He won't be happy with me.

- To be a godly woman you must have good relationships with everyone you know. If there is a problem, it must be fixed. If it is not, it's your fault.

- I am not as good as anyone else.

- I will always be the way I am. I can't change.

- You always learn from pain. Illustration below.

  1. If I am a good little girl, my daddy won't drink. I know I am the cause of this. No one tells me that I am. It's just something I know in my mind. (Age seven.)

  2. If I have sex with guys they will fall in love me and I will live happily ever after. (Age eighteen.)

  3. If I apologize to my husband every time he does something wrong, I will be considered submissive. (Age thirty.)

  4. If I have sex with guys, they will fall in love with me, and I will live happily ever after. (Age forty-five.) Slow learner!

And so it goes. The myths are many, but you can see that they cover our wounds like dirty Band-Aids. The implications of these myths are huge for us as Christian women. If we believe even one of these, then we have at least one link of the chain of bondage that we drag around with us no matter what we do. It cripples us. It is heavy, and it causes us to live life at a lower level than our precious Father intends for us.

WHERE IS IT WRITTEN?

I believe that any woman who wants to live the full, abundant life Jesus offers needs some tools in order to come out from under the myths that cause her misery. If you are going to dream of a "new day," you need a way to get there! You need some questions that, like a master key, will open the doors behind which the myths are stored. And if you are a women who is willing to challenge your belief system in order to find peace and freedom, one of the best questions you can ask is, "Where is it written?"

Of course, if you ask the question, you have to be the one willing to seek the answer. You will find that there are many myth-makers who have an interest in maintaining the status quo for you. They will be more than willing to show you Scriptures, pulling out texts to prove their point. Too many of us have been too satisfied with that kind of "study" for too long. It is our responsibility, my sister, to dig out our own answers so that we might be confident in what we believe. The Holy Spirit was given to us to "lead us into all truth." He will be our teacher as we inquire *honestly*, "Where is it written?"

During my adult life, one of the biggest messes I ever got into took place because I had a friend who believed a myth about friendship. Somewhere along the line she had put together a formula for being a good friend, and she clung to it faithfully. It was an intense, demanding, consuming formula. When I questioned some of her reasoning, she immediately became defensive and told me I knew nothing about friendship and only understood shallow relationships. Needless to say, I was stunned. I thought I had pretty good relationships, but if there was something I didn't know and had missed, I was open to learning.

Foolishly and unarmed with my defining question, "Where is it written?" I fell for her formula hook, line, and the proverbial sinker. The only problem was that her understanding of friendship was defined only in her head from her experience. Because of her bruised and broken background, her ideas could have been a primer for codependency. Because I didn't go to the Scriptures and earnestly ask the question, "Where is it written?" I ended up in a relational mess. I believed a myth without questioning and paid a steep price in the process.

Of course, I stayed in the relationship, trying to be a friend by her definition but failing on a regular basis. I was miserable, and I made other friends miserable because I was trying to prove the veracity of a myth—and it was causing chaos in my life and in theirs, too. I should have played heads-up at the first red flag. Why wasn't my way working? When you find that you are living by some questionable code of behavior, it is best to keep asking yourself questions. After you ask that first question, "Where is it written?" it is a good idea to ask yourself, "Is what I am believing working?" Truth sets you free, and truth works. It may be hard to apply, and it may challenge you to be bigger and better than you are, but truth will not leave you swirling in a quagmire. It will never leave you feeling stuck and hopeless.

I finally reached the point where the confusion was too great, the results too disappointing. The friendship was too weak to survive. I failed to put what I was being told through the grid of "Where is it written?" and "Is what I am doing working?" This was a costly mistake for me, and it is costly for anyone who is caught in a situation that is going nowhere and seems to have no answers. I assure you that if you will have the courage to begin to question, you will find answers. You may not like what you find, but you will see what is needed to bring stability to your own soul, even though it may be hard.

WHY DO WE FAIL TO QUESTION?

Recently I had dinner with several old friends who were discussing the behavior of their adult children. They were dismayed over the young people's lack of self-respect and personal goals. The lament was great as these mothers spoke of grown children who seemingly had no desire to change. They were stuck in dead-end jobs and destructive relationships, but instead of moving, were just vegetating. As I listened, I could not help thinking of the decisions the mothers had made over the years. In fact, I thought of the decisions they had failed to make, decisions to question the relationships they had with their husbands. Each of the men had consistently demonstrated emotional immaturity and had been abusive to their wives and children. So they also were stuck. They were unhappy but covered it over by drinking and playing games. Their behavior had been expected, accepted, and ignored by their wives. If asked, the wives probably would have said that they had made peace with their husbands' behavior. The wives were OK with where they were. They had found ways to compensate. Life went on.

The only problem was that there was a generation of children growing up in the unquestioned shadow of the fathers. The mothers accepted the status quo, and the fathers' behavior went unchallenged. Now the children were wondering, "What am I to believe?" "How am I to live?"

Was there a myth that was believed?

Was there a truth that was ignored?

What had happened?

The mothers didn't question what was happening because that didn't "feel right." They asked, "Won't time take care of everything?" And then they replied, "Well, of course. I heard that somewhere, and surely it is true."

It may be too late to start raising questions in your primary relationship, but it is never too late to question yourself. It may mean a late course correction that is as small as writing a letter asking forgiveness for causing pain. You may be unable to change the nature of the primary relationship, but at least those who have been hurt by it can be acknowledged and validated. They can hear their mother say, "I was wrong to let you go through what we went through as a family. I thought there was nothing to do. I was discontent, and now I know it was a discontent I needed to question. I am sorry for your sakes that I didn't do it before now."

What kind of an impact could that have in the life of a wounded adult child?

What difference could it bring to the wife and mother who has awakened to a better way?

What kind of impact could it have on the self-satisfied mate?

From Dan Allender's book *The Healing Path,* again:

Take the wife who admits her marriage is a tiresome moral sham. As she hungers for more, facing her fears and demands, she will struggle with the log in her own eye but will also refuse to allow sameness to remain the pattern for the rest of her marriage. To admit discontent and hunger for redemption requires that we face our part in the problem and compels us to yearn and dream of more.

Conversely, a person without hope accepts her present circumstance as inevitable. It simply has to be endured. No wonder endurance is often the trademark of the self-righteous. They live in unendurable situations with no complaint, no demands. In fact, the self-righteous live with now acknowledged, confessed desire. . . . The martyr in each of us refuses holy discontent. We would prefer to retreat in furious, uncompromising silence rather than face our need for someone to rescue us or at least join us in our helplessness.[2]

Think about what Allender has said. Then accept this personal challenge:

If you want to become a person who is willing to question herself, take time right now to write down a problem that has plagued you for longer than you would like to admit. Write out what you have done about the problem to date and why you have done it that way. Ask yourself, "Is what I am doing working? If it is not, why not? Where is it written that I must continue to deal with the problem this way?"

Take some time to think through what God is saying to you here. His word is clear. He doesn't mumble or play games. In the course of reading this book and dealing with these myths, take up this personal challenge regularly. Then read Psalms 26 and 27, given below. As you read, underline the phrases that jump out at you and meditate (chew) on them. Ask God, "What do you want me to learn?" I believe you will begin to see an incredible revelation of the heart of God. You will see more clearly as your mind and heart are tested and you become determined that it can be said of you: "She has walked in integrity (completeness, fullness, simplicity, and innocence)." What a goal!

⁓PSALM 26⁓
A PSALM OF DAVID.

Vindicate me, O LORD, for I have walked in my integrity,
And I have trusted in the LORD without wavering.
Examine me, O LORD, and try me;
Test my mind and my heart.
For Your lovingkindness is before my eyes,
And I have walked in Your truth.
I do not sit with deceitful men,
Nor will I go with pretenders.
I hate the assembly of evildoers,
And I will not sit with the wicked.

I shall wash my hands in innocence,
And I will go about Your altar, O LORD,
That I may proclaim with the voice of thanksgiving
And declare all Your wonders.

O LORD, I love the habitation of Your house
And the place where Your glory dwells.
Do not take my soul away along with sinners,
Nor my life with men of bloodshed,
In whose hands is a wicked scheme,
And whose right hand is full of bribes.
But as for me, I shall walk in my integrity;
Redeem me, and be gracious to me.
My foot stands on a level place;
In the congregations I shall bless the LORD.

—PSALM 27—
A PSALM OF DAVID.

The LORD is my light and my salvation;
Whom shall I fear?
The LORD is the defense of my life;
Whom shall I dread?
When evildoers came upon me to devour my flesh,
My adversaries and my enemies, they stumbled and fell.
Though a host encamp against me,
My heart will not fear;
Though war arise against me,
In spite of this I shall be confident.

One thing I have asked from the LORD, that I shall seek:
That I may dwell in the house of the LORD all the days of my life,
To behold the beauty of the LORD
And to meditate in His temple.
For in the day of trouble He will conceal me in His tabernacle;
In the secret place of His tent He will hide me;
He will lift me up on a rock.
And now my head will be lifted up above my enemies around me,
And I will offer in His tent sacrifices with shouts of joy;

I will sing, yes, I will sing praises to the LORD.
Hear, O LORD, when I cry with my voice,
And be gracious to me and answer me.
When You said, "Seek My face," my heart said to You,
"Your face, O LORD, I shall seek."
Do not hide Your face from me,
Do not turn Your servant away in anger;
You have been my help;
Do not abandon me nor forsake me,
O God of my salvation!
For my father and my mother have forsaken me,
But the LORD will take me up.

Teach me Your way, O LORD,
And lead me in a level path
Because of my foes.
Do not deliver me over to the desire of my adversaries,
For false witnesses have risen against me,
And such as breathe out violence.
I would have despaired unless I had believed that I would see

the goodness of the LORD
In the land of the living.
Wait for the LORD*;*
Be strong and let your heart take courage;
Yes, wait for the LORD.

MYTHS
IN THE
GARDEN

How could they have ended up in this predicament? The morning started out so beautifully. The pomegranates were particularly delicious . . . the grapes tasted like the finest jewels of the garden . . . the birds chirped cheerfully . . . the brook provided them with fresh, bubbling water, and the gentle breeze caressed their nude bodies. The sun had warmed them with a perfect glow as they lay in a glen with their heads propped on the sides of the two woolly sheep that followed them everywhere. If the man and the woman were running down a garden path, there were the sheep. If the man and the woman stopped to rest, the sheep would be their pillows. The lions followed at a distance with pure hearts toward the sheep, as well as toward the man and the woman, while the gentle giraffes munched on the tops of the trees. The animals were their friends, companions, and entertainment. They were always there to make the lives of the man and the woman more enjoyable, as if it could get any better.

How could a few short hours, a brief conversation, and one little bite of fruit land them here? Now they were cold. They were angry—

angry at one another, angry at what has happened, and angry that Lord God obviously has turned His back and abandoned them.

The loneliness was unreal. They had never felt anything like it. How, oh, how could this be?

It all happened after the serpent casually strolled into the garden and started a simple conversation with the woman. "Has God said?" That's the way it began.

EVE

The serpent said to the woman, "You surely will not die! For God knows that in the day you eat from it your eyes will be opened, and you will be like God, knowing good and evil." (GENESIS 3:4–5)

From the moment he made the suggestion, doubt began to hover around Eve's heart like a wreath of smoke. "Has God said?" Then came the stunning statement from the beautiful created being, "You surely shall not die!" She jerked her head as the thought hit her. *That* is what had kept them away from the tree, the tree with the gorgeous fruit. Lord God didn't want them to have it. It was so beautiful and they would have so much more. In fact, as she thought about it, Lord God didn't even want them to touch it.

ADAM

With a dull thud the myth sunk into her being. Satan had made his suggestion. Eve thought about it long enough to make it reasonable in her head. Now she really thought it was true, so true that she turned to Adam and made a myth-believer out of him.

"Adam, you know we won't die if we eat of the Tree of Knowledge of Good and Evil. It won't happen. God just doesn't want us to be like Him. That's what all that is about. He wants to keep us locked into depending on Him for everything and believing that there is some big consequence when we do what we want to do. Adam, that just isn't true. He doesn't mean what He says. Why would He let us die? He just created us. That is so silly, and besides that, Adam, I think He is holding out on us! We could be like Him but He doesn't want us to know everything He knows or have the power He has. I think that is so selfish of Lord God. So, Adam, think about it. Look at that fruit. What's wrong with eating just a bite? He won't care. You can do what you want to, but I am going to get what I have coming. Somebody has to make things happen around here. It's obvious that you aren't, and neither is He. I'm going to eat. Come on . . ."

Oh, what a huge blunder believing that myth turned out to be. *God is holding out on us, and He doesn't mean what He says.* Immediately, blame, shame, and guilt began springing up in the garden.

THE COUPLE

A sense of restlessness invaded Paradise as the first couple realized the altered state in which they now found themselves. Hurried sewing of leaves to make loin coverings occupied their frenzied attention. They didn't notice the chill in the air. They were busy, and it was imperceptible at first. The temperature seemed to have dropped ten degrees before they felt it. Then, before they could get comfortable with the unfamiliar leafy loin coverings, there was the voice, the voice that always came in the cool of the day.

"Where are you?"

Adam answered, "I heard the sound of You in the garden, and I was afraid because I was naked; so I hid myself."

"Who told you that you were naked? What is this you have done?"

The voice of Lord God was filled with greater pain, sadness, and outrage with each question He asked.

"We are naked . . ."

The human voices became smaller and weaker as they stammered quiet little answers.

"The woman you gave me . . ."

"The serpent gave me to eat . . ."

Then the noticeable shrillness of the large swans and peacocks began to intensify. The rage of the crickets and the anxiety of the nursing cattle began to be heard as never before in the Garden.

Things were not right in Paradise.

And everyone knew it.

"Who told you that you were naked? Have you eaten from the

tree of which I commanded you not to eat?"

Everybody had his whining say before Lord God, and then there was a moment of quiet.

SATAN

I can imagine that at this point the serpent thought, "Now is a good time for me to leave." He was, no doubt, gleefully watching the agony and pain he had caused for the Creator and His precious created ones. He had done enough for now. Time to be going!

All that could be heard was the rustle of leaves as he divided the foliage to make his exit.

The voice was deliberate as God thundered: *"You!"*

> *"Because you have done this,*
> *Cursed are you more than all cattle,*
> *And more than every beast of the field;*
> *On your belly you will go,*
> *And dust you will eat*
> *All the days of your life;*
> *And I will put enmity*
> *Between you and the woman,*
> *And between your seed and her seed;*
> *He shall bruise you on the head,*
> *And you shall bruise him on the heel."*
>
> ⁓ GENESIS 3:14–15

With that decree, the serpent, who had come on the scene so full of himself, so arrogant, so determined to rise above the Most High, now found himself writhing through the dirt as he hurried to make his shameful exit. The promise, "He will bruise you on the head," boomed out over him. He was low now, as low as he had ever been. He knew the One who would bruise his head would have authority over him. Oh, he could bruise His heel, but what kind of wound was that? He knew One who would finish him off was coming from the seed of the woman. He knew that Lord God had just sentenced him to a state of perdition. He knew it was over, but he left with a deadly determination not to be the only one to crawl through the dirt. He would bring down with himself everyone he possibly could.

He had a plan. It had worked in this place. It would work again. He had no doubt of that! Just make a suggestion. Just create a little doubt. "'God is holding out on you, and God doesn't mean what He says.' That's it. Easiest work I'll ever have do. Oh, I may have my legs cut out from under me, but there is no way I will totally be defeated. I can still lie, I can still steal, I can still destroy. I am still Satan."

EVE'S SENTENCE

The rustling sound grew faint as Lord God turned to the woman.

"You will have pain in childbirth like no pain you have ever known. Your desire shall be for your husband, and he will rule over you." (GENESIS 3:16, PARAPHRASE)

The sentence was short, to the point, and life changing. Eve's greatest joy would hold the potential of her greatest sorrow. Not only would her body be ripped and thrown into spasms she had never known just to bring forth her children, but after their birth, they would always have a hold on her heart. Some would make her heart swell with joy while others would break it. She didn't yet know that one of her son's would murder the other. She couldn't know, yet. All she knew was what Lord God had said, and it disturbed her. He added that her desire would be for her husband. Her need to be deeply intimate with him would keep her in tension as she tried to relate to him. Things were different now from what they had been. She longed for Adam's adoring touch, but he was receiving the news from Lord God about his new life. He had a new role—he would "rule over her."

Eve wrapped her arms around herself and sobbed, "What have I done?"

She looked at Adam with a pout on her lips, crying, "Why did you listen, why did you listen? This really is your fault."

ADAM'S SENTENCE

Adam stood with his head hanging. What would Lord God say to him?

> *"Because you have listened to the voice of your wife, and have*
> *eaten from the tree about which I commanded you, saying,*
> *'You shall not eat from it';*
> *Cursed is the ground because of you;*
> *In toil you will eat of it*
> *All the days of your life.*
> *Both thorns and thistles it shall grow for you;*
> *And you will eat the plants of the field;*
> *By the sweat of your face*
> *You will eat bread,*
> *Till you return to the ground,*
> *Because from it you were taken;*
> *For you are dust,*
> *And to dust you shall return."*
> — GENESIS 3:17 –19

Tears of rage and shame dropped on Adam's chest. He didn't know who to blame the most—Eve, who had first brought up the subject; himself for eating; or Lord God for being too right, too strong, too tough.

Couldn't Lord God have a little mercy?

Couldn't He just throw a rewind button back to morning? Could they not have a second chance?

Could He prove He meant what He said, maybe with some sort of sign or something? Could He prove He wasn't holding out on them by letting them escape His judgment just this once? Maybe He could show them what He had in store for them? Maybe Lord God could just forget about all of this and let us start again. . . .

AFTERMATH

But, no. It was too late. Everything was happening too fast. The cool of the day had moved too quickly to the chill of evening. A cold, dank fog was rising from the river and crawling toward the man and his wife. They stood huddled together like abandoned children. They felt disposed of, alone, bewildered, and full of shame. They kept pulling at the fig leaves, trying to make them fit, but it never seemed to work. Then, just as they thought maybe Lord God had forgotten them, "The LORD God made garments of skin for Adam and his wife, and clothed them" (Genesis 3:21).

In horror they looked down at their bodies, now covered with the skins of the sheep that had been their companions that morning. They felt warm blood beginning to cool and stick to their bodies as Lord God clothed them and covered their nakedness. They couldn't believe that something innocent had to die just because they had eaten one bite of fruit. What did Lord God mean by all of this?

They clutched the skins to themselves, seeking warmth but repulsed by the blood that stuck to them. They looked on the ground and recognized the severed heads of the two sheep that had followed them everywhere, who had been their companions. They saw the staring, vacant, dead eyes that once had looked back at them with playful adoration. It was over now. The sheep were dead. The carefree days of innocence were gone. The burden of Lord God's merciful rejection was about to fall on them, and they had no defense. The serpent had left long ago. All that was left of him was a sinuous trail in the dirt, the only sign that he had even been there.

Then they heard the words that would haunt them the rest of their days. Every time they remembered the garden, they remembered this scene. They remembered the feel of the sheep's blood against their skin and the feeling of betrayal that hung heavy in the air.

In their shame they wondered, "How could we betray the animals? How could we betray each other? How could we betray Lord God?" They were inconsolable, and yet they stood as far apart as they had ever been. How could you turn to someone who had gotten you into this mess and expect him to comfort you?

While they were clutching the skins close to themselves, they heard Lord God speak again:

> *"Behold, the man has become like one of Us, knowing good and evil; and now, he might stretch out his hand, and take also from the tree of life, and eat, and live forever."* (GENESIS 3:22)

The voice of Lord God did not complete that sentence. Now that they knew the difference between good and evil, if they lived forever there would be no escape, and evil would only abound more and more. If they didn't die . . . the thought was monstrous beyond contemplation.

> *Therefore the LORD God sent him out from the garden of Eden, to cultivate the ground from which he was taken. So He drove the man out; and at the east of the garden of Eden He stationed the cherubim and the flaming sword which turned every direction to guard the way to the tree of life.* (GENESIS 3:23–24)

It was hard to sleep that night. The ground was hard, cold, stony. There was no plump sheep for a pillow. They had to use every bit of the skin to cover themselves. There was no soft spot for their heads. As they lay back to back, more for warmth than for any closeness they felt, Eve began to whimper, "Adam, I'm hungry."

She had never known hunger in this way before.

"In the garden," she said to Adam, "I always had something to eat. When are you going to start planting our food? I could starve waiting on you."

Adam's jaw tightened as he responded to her childish whine. "If you had just minded your own . . . ah, forget it. You'll just have to get by on roots and grass until I can do something with this dirt."

He felt Eve's body shake with sobs. No words came out of her mouth. He had nothing more to say, but neither of them could sleep, for in the distance they saw the glow of the mighty flaming sword turning back and forth. Their minds kept going back to the morning. "Was it only this morning that we got up and the pomegranates and the grapes were ripe and waiting for breakfast? Was it only this morning

36

we walked down to the glen and the sheep went with us? Was it only this morning we lay our heads on their sides and laughed and laughed? Was it only this morning we held hands? Was it only this morning?"

Oh, the power of the myth that God doesn't mean what He says, and that God is holding out on you.

IT DIDN'T END WITH ADAM AND EVE

Adam and Eve have their counterparts in life today. People from all walks of life make the same mistake the first couple did—and reap the consequences.

- Brock and Joanna sat in the attorney's office in a hushed silence. Joanna had filed for divorce from Brock because he had done some pretty unbelievably stupid things with their money. He had been so scared that they would not have enough to put their kids through college that he had invested their life's savings in a scheme that left them penniless. Brock was a good man, but he had recklessly taken matters into his own hands when responsibility began to squeeze in on him. Joanna did the same thing. If Brock was going to be so reckless, how on earth could she stay married to him? She had had it! The irony? Brock was a pastor and Joanna taught Sunday school. They knew what God said and they knew that they were in a mess, but they never quite got to the core of the problem. Neither of them believed that God meant what He said, and both of them believed in the recesses of their hearts that God was holding out on them. Consequently, they took matters into their own hands, blamed each other, and wrecked their lives.

- Danielle was a bitter forty-year-old woman. All she had wanted was a husband and a family. Why had God withheld a husband from her? She went to church but she had an edge, a bitter edge that announced, "God's holding out on me, and God doesn't mean what He says."

- Ginger was living in a lesbian lifestyle. She hated to hear people at her church even mention the word "homosexuality." What did they know? She was the one who knew she was different. She was the one who knew God had made her that way, so how could He condemn what she did? She went to church because she loved the Lord and absolutely could not believe that He did not approve of the way she was living. After all, isn't a loving relationship what it is all about? She would agree that her heart had been broken a couple of times by lovers who had left her, but her "hetero" girlfriends at work had their hearts broken, too. What's the big deal?

- When Gerry's son became ill with a debilitating muscular disease when he was only twenty-nine, she turned her back on God. How could God allow her son to go through this terrible disease? How could she possibly trust a God who would allow her to hurt so? If all that stuff they sang was true, then it was true for someone else. It surely didn't apply in her case.

- Donna was a beautiful young woman who was abused by her father when she was a very young girl. When she reached adulthood, she was angry, promiscuous, and hungry for love. She wanted a relationship with God because there were some women at work who obviously lived at peace and seemed joyful all the time. But every time they got into one of those discussions, Donna would blow up and ask the same question, "If there is a God, why did He let me go through all of that stuff with my father? Why is he getting by with denying he ever did a thing and I am the one who hurts every day?"

Each of these women was making the same assumptions Adam and Eve had made: "God is holding out on me, and God doesn't mean what He says." They believed a myth, and consequently, the peace, joy, and contentment that could be theirs were blocked. They wanted a relationship with God, but they couldn't get past what they believed about Him.

That is the problem for many of us. We want a relationship with Him, we want what we see other people experiencing, but because of what we believe about Him, we are blocked.

God just doesn't act consistently with what we believe. It is so easy for us—like Adam and Eve—to think that if He doesn't carry through the way we think He should, He doesn't mean what He says. It is easier for us to think that if He doesn't give us what we ask for and think we just have to have, He is holding out on us.

GOD DOESN'T YELL "CUT" BEFORE DANGER COMES

Brent Curtis and John Eldredge write in *The Sacred Romance:*

When we were young, most of us loved adventure. There is something about the unknown that draws us, which is why we like stories so much. But I like to leave the theater at the end of the play, knowing that the dilemma of evil has been resolved by the characters on the stage or screen . . . to find ourselves not as spectators but as central characters in the play itself is somewhat daunting. The stakes are truly high, sometimes literally life or death, and God rarely, if ever, yells "Cut!" just as the dangerous or painful scene descends upon us. No stunt doubles come onto the set to take our places. Many of us feel that we have been playing these kinds of scenes ever since we were children. We wonder if the hero will ever show up to rescue us.

We would like to picture goodness as being synonymous with safety. When we think of God being good, we perhaps picture someone like Al on the popular TV program, *Home Improvement.* He is someone who carefully plans out each task ahead of time and has all the proper tools and safety equipment in place; someone who has thought out every possible danger ahead of time and makes allowances to ensure our safety as his workmate; someone who goes to bed early, gets plenty of rest and wears flannel shirts as a mark of his reliability.

Being in partnership with God, though, often feels much more like being Mel Gibson's sidekick in the movie *Lethal Weapon.* In his determination to deal with the bad guys, he leaps from seventh-story balconies into swimming pools, surprised that we would have any hesitation in following after him. Like Indiana Jones' love interest in the movies, we find ourselves caught up in an adventure of heroic proportions with a God who both seduces us with his boldness and energy and repels us with his willingness to place us in mortal danger, suspended over pits of snakes.[1]

GOD'S PLACE OF SAFETY IS TO TRUST AND OBEY

The spin-off of the myth we get caught up in is that God is supposed to act the way we do. He is supposed to think like we do, and the only way we can trust Him is if He behaves the way we think He should. That puts God in a cage for us to observe and figure out. He repeatedly refutes that notion by telling us things such as this:

> *"For My thoughts are not your thoughts,*
> *Nor are your ways My ways," declares the* LORD.
> *"For as the heavens are higher than the earth,*
> *So are My ways higher than your ways*
> *And My thoughts than your thoughts."*
> — ISAIAH 55:8–9

> *The secret of the Lord is for those who fear Him,*
> *And He will make them know His covenant.*
> — PSALM 25:14

Yet even when we read these passages, we keep coming back to the myth. The whispering liar suggests that if God doesn't act the way we think He should, then He doesn't mean what He says. And, not only that, He is holding out on us. Never mind that the Scripture is clear:

> *For the* LORD *God is a sun and shield;*
> *The* LORD *gives grace and glory;*
> *No good thing does He withhold from those who walk uprightly.*
> *O* LORD *of hosts,*
> *How blessed is the man who trusts in You!*
> — PSALM 84:11–12

It is easier to believe the myth because we base our assessment of God on what we would do or how we would behave in a given situation. We want to make God into our image rather than the other way around. When we are desperate, we want God to step up to the plate and "act like a man"—and yet that is not our God. He has given the same simple message from the beginning: *Trust and obey Me; therein is your safety.*

If we believe the myth, then we move from the place of safety, where we rely on Him, to the place of danger, where we rely on ourselves and our own understanding of how things should be. This is a giant leap over an extremely dangerous chasm that we make without a safety net.

There is only one place of safety. It was Eve's place. It is your place. It is my place. It is every person's safe place, the place of trust that says, "I will choose to believe that You mean what You say. Even if it does not make any logical sense to me and even if I don't like it, I will choose to believe You mean what You say because ultimately You will show me that it is for my good that You have said it! I have to trust that."

The second tier of safety is the place where you dare to believe God is not holding out on you even though you may *feel* as if He is. Like Job, you may be at the bottom, but remember, he had a place of safety based on trust.

"Be silent before me so that I may speak;
Then let come on me what may.
Why should I take my flesh in my teeth
And put my life in my hands?
Though He slay me,
I will hope in Him.
Nevertheless I will argue my ways before Him.
This also will be my salvation,
For a godless man may not come before His presence.
Listen carefully to my speech,
And let my declaration fill your ears.

41

Behold now, I have prepared my case;
I know that I will be vindicated.
Who will contend with me?
For then I would be silent and die.

"Only two things do not do to me,
Then I will not hide from Your face:
Remove Your hand from me,
And let not the dread of You terrify me.
Then call, and I will answer;
Or let me speak, then reply to me."

⸺ JOB 13:13–22

The choice belongs to you. If you want the security of knowing that God means what He says and that He is not holding out on you, then you will have to train your mind to believe it to be true even though your eyes might give you a different message.

Myths feed on perceptions, not on truth. The Word of God is truth; therefore, when you want to be set free from the bondage of the myth, you must retrain your brain to think truth rather than perception. It becomes an issue of faith, not sight! Faith is taking God at His word. Sight is what you see. Your sight is always subject to perception. It is how you see things that counts.

As you begin the retraining process, meditate on Psalm 91 every day for a month. Read it silently, read it aloud, rewrite it in your own words, and eventually memorize it so that you can recall it at a moment's notice. You will be amazed how the myths become dimmer in your mind as you brighten your path with the truth of God's Word. Can you read this psalm and really believe the myth that God's holding out on you and God doesn't mean what He says? I really don't think so!

‒PSALM 91‒
SECURITY OF THE ONE WHO TRUSTS IN THE LORD.

He who dwells in the shelter of the Most High
Will abide in the shadow of the Almighty.
I will say to the LORD, *"My refuge and my fortress,*
My God, in whom I trust!"
For it is He who delivers you from the snare of the trapper
And from the deadly pestilence.
He will cover you with His pinions,
And under His wings you may seek refuge;
His faithfulness is a shield and bulwark.

You will not be afraid of the terror by night,
Or of the arrow that flies by day;
Of the pestilence that stalks in darkness,
Or of the destruction that lays waste at noon.
A thousand may fall at your side
And ten thousand at your right hand,
But it shall not approach you.
You will only look on with your eyes
And see the recompense of the wicked.
For you have made the LORD, *my refuge,*
Even the Most High, your dwelling place.
No evil will befall you,
Nor will any plague come near your tent.

For He will give His angels charge concerning you,
To guard you in all your ways.
They will bear you up in their hands,
That you do not strike your foot against a stone.
You will tread upon the lion and cobra,
The young lion and the serpent you will trample down.

43

"Because he has loved Me, therefore I will deliver him;
I will set him securely on high, because he has known My name.
"He will call upon Me, and I will answer him;
I will be with him in trouble;
I will rescue him and honor him.
"With a long life I will satisfy him
And let him see My salvation."

If He meant what He said to Adam and Eve, "On the day that you eat thereof, you shall surely die," then He means what has told us through the psalmist.

"Because he has loved Me, therefore I will deliver him;
I will set him securely on high, because he has known My name.
He will call upon Me, and I will answer him;
I will be with him in trouble;
I will rescue him and honor him.
With a long life I will satisfy him
And let him see My salvation."

Truth is truth and a myth is a myth. I choose to believe that God means what He says in both places and that His heart is never to hold out on you or me!

THE MYTH
OF
DAMAGED
GOODS

T his is a subtle one. Women you would never suspect in a million years believe it. They are up-front, popular, bright, attractive, and full of charm, but there is a gray cloud in the back of their minds. It is the myth of damaged goods, and it sends the paralyzing message, "You aren't good enough." "Good enough for what?" would be a good reply, but I haven't found many women who are willing to stop and think through this nebulous feeling.

Historically, we as women have been viewed as "less than" because we are different. God obviously created women to be different from men, but nowhere in Scripture do we find that He views woman as any more flawed than man—we are just flawed in different ways. Tragically, man and woman incurred their own damage when they tangled with the serpent in the Garden of Eden. Both received hard but redemptive punishment for believing the Evil One's deceitful suggestions. Although the redemptive plan is in place today, the Enemy still is busy lying and deceiving. He continued his truth twisting after he crawled out of the Garden on his belly. The pride-killing curse he received in

Genesis 3 seemed only to make him more determined to "kill, steal, and destroy" (see John 10:10). Consequently, women have suffered his myth-spreading woes since the beginning.

EARLY CULTURAL MYTHS ABOUT WOMEN

In an article excerpted from *Compton's Interactive Encyclopedia,* the Women's International Center Web site observes:

> Since early times women have been uniquely viewed as a creative source of human life. Historically, however, they have been considered not only intellectually inferior to men but also a major source of temptation and evil. In Greek mythology, for example, it was a woman, Pandora, who opened the forbidden box and brought plagues and unhappiness to mankind. Early Roman law described women as children, forever inferior to men.
>
> Early Christian theology perpetuated these views. St. Jerome, a 4th-century Latin father of the church, said: "Woman is the gate of the devil, the path of wickedness, the sting of the serpent, in a word a perilous object." Thomas Aquinas, the 13th-century Christian theologian, said that woman was "created to be man's helpmeet, but her unique role is in conception . . . since for other purposes men would be better assisted by other men."[1]

Marie Chapian writes in *A Confident, Dynamic You*:

> In earlier times the only way a woman could serve the Lord with all her gifts was to join an order of nuns. Between A.D. 100 and A.D. 500 women were drawn to the ascetic life of contemplation and prayer because life in the convent offered a woman freedom to worship the Lord and find her identity in her relationship to him. Her only other option in life was to marry and have children, often with a man not of her own choosing.
>
> Martin Luther's views on the inferiority of women are no secret. The Reformers as a whole held that women existed for the comfort and well-being of men. Calvin, for instance, explained to friends what he wanted in a woman: "A woman who is gentle, pure, modest, economical, patient and is likely to interest herself about my health."[2]

JESUS' VIEW OF WOMEN

Attitudes permeate the environment, and it is easy to pick up the thought that being female is "less than." In Jesus' day, it was no different. The people who had sat in darkness for four hundred years before He came included women, who were viewed as property by their husbands. The darkness of their world was a reflection of the darkness of the times. And then Jesus came on the scene. He brought a dignity to women that directly challenged the pharisaic religious culture of His day. It was a religious system where the common prayer among some of the religious leaders was, "I thank God I was not born a Gentile, a woman, or a dog!" (Pretty good company for us girls, I'd say!)

Jesus had an agenda when he started His ministry. A strong part of that agenda was to bring freedom from bigotry. Imagine yourself sitting in the corner of the synagogue the day that Jesus stood to read near the beginning of His earthly ministry.

> *And Jesus returned to Galilee in the power of the Spirit, and news about Him spread through all the surrounding district.*
>
> *And He began teaching in their synagogues and was praised by all.*
>
> *And He came to Nazareth, where He had been brought up; and as was His custom, He entered the synagogue on the Sabbath, and stood up to read.*
>
> *And the book of the prophet Isaiah was handed to Him. And He opened the book and found the place where it was written,*
>
> *"The Spirit of the* LORD *is upon Me,*
>
> *Because He anointed Me to preach the gospel to the poor.*
>
> *He has sent Me to proclaim release to the captives,*
>
> *And recovery of sight to the blind,*
>
> *To set free those who are oppressed,*
>
> *To proclaim the favorable year of the* LORD.*"*
>
> *And He closed the book, gave it back to the attendant and sat down; and the eyes of all in the synagogue were fixed on Him.* (LUKE 4:14–20)

Jesus had come to release the captives and to offer freedom to the oppressed. Women were some of the very people He had come to set free. He was an enigma to those who watched. To those who were satisfied with their grip on power, He was a threat to the old system, the system that gave them security. To some, including many women, He was the light at the end of the tunnel, the hope of the ages, and the promised Messiah, and they had no intention of letting their culture keep them from Him. He had brought the first good news they ever had heard! He made women believe they were worth something.

Several of these women appear by name in the Gospels: Joanna, the wife of Chuza (Luke 8:3; 24:10); Susanna (Luke 8:3); Mary, the mother of James and Joses (Matthew 27:56; Mark 15:40; Luke 24:10); Salome (Mark 15:40); and the wife of Zebedee and the mother of James and John (Matthew 27:56; see also Matthew 20:20–24).[3]

> In addition to [these women] the writers state clearly that "many" other women followed Jesus (for example, see Matt. 27:55; Mark 15:41; Luke 8:3; [24:1, 10]). Luke indicates that women provided materially for Jesus and the disciples—a curious statement in that Jewish women of the time generally did not have much control over their families' resources. Nor did women commonly travel with a rabbi. . . . Indeed, strict codes tended to distance Jewish leaders from women, so much so that by Jesus' time a rabbi was not even to speak to his wife in public.
>
> But Jesus apparently thought little of such taboos. There is no indication that He discouraged women from being His followers. They listened to His teaching, accompanied Him in His travels, stood by Him at His crucifixion, gave witness to His resurrection, and eventually helped spread His message throughout the Roman world.[4]

Mary Magdalene was also among those women.

> The Gospels mention Mary of Magdala by name more than any other female disciple. One reason may be the dramatic turnaround in her life that the Lord brought about by casting out seven demons. She responded by supporting His ministry and joining with several other women who traveled with Him (Luke 8:1–3).
>
> Mary's loyalty proved unwavering right to the end. While the Twelve fled after Jesus' arrest, Mary stood by at His crucifixion (Matt. 27:56; Mark 15:40; John 19:25). She also helped prepare His body for burial (Matt. 27:61; Mark 15:47; Luke 23:55). Perhaps it was to reward her

undying devotion that the Lord allowed her to be the first person to meet Him after the resurrection (Mark 16:9–10; John 20:14–18).[5]

> *Now after He had risen early on the first day of the week, He first appeared to Mary Magdalene, from whom He had cast out seven demons. She went and reported to those who had been with Him, while they were mourning and weeping. When they heard that He was alive and had been seen by her, they refused to believe it.* (MARK 16:9–11)

Curiously, however, the disciples refused to believe Mary's report of the risen Lord. In fact, they dismissed it as an "idle tale" (Mark 16:11; Luke 24:11). Perhaps their skepticism betrayed long-held doubts about Mary's credibility: after all, hadn't she been possessed by seven demons? Moreover, Jewish culture raised its men to consider the testimony of women as inferior.

Nevertheless, Jesus chose Mary to report the good news of His resurrection to His other followers. Later, He rebuked them for their unwillingness to believe her (Mark 16:14).[6]

> *Afterward He appeared to the eleven themselves as they were reclining at the table; and He reproached them for their unbelief and hardness of heart, because they had not believed those who had seen Him after He had risen.* (MARK 16:14)

Thanks to Him, she was a changed person. Moreover, she was a reliable witness, having proven her trustworthiness through her perseverance and steadfastness in the face of danger and doubt.[7]

Amazing Mary Magdalene had every reason to feel like damaged goods. She had been healed of seven demons, and usually there were physical manifestations with demon possession—speechlessness (Matthew 9:33), violence (Matthew 8:28), blindness (Matthew 12:22), convulsions (Mark 1:26), or foaming at the mouth (Luke 9:39). Jesus healed her of demon possession, but would the people around her see her as a "new creation"? Maybe yes, maybe no. That did not stop her. Every time Jesus turned around, the adoring, self-assured Mary Magdalene was there! She had met Jesus, and she would never be the same.

So, although her culture failed to recognize the God-given value and position of a woman, she was undaunted. Jesus delivered her, recognized her value, and expected others to see her for who she was—not for what she used to be. He saw her as a valuable individual, not as someone who was "less than" because of her gender or past. Because she knew and believed this, she acted like a whole person. She refused to wrap herself in the myth perpetrated by her culture. If it did not see her as a whole person, so be it. Jesus did, and that was enough for her.

Lisa is a twentieth-century Mary Magdalene. She has never had recognizable demons, but she has a past that would make most church folks blush. Those who know her question her sanity from time to time, but she just plugs on, loving Jesus, trusting Him to take care of her and her children, basking in His forgiveness, and gratefully rejoicing in the life she has been given. Amazingly, she does not see herself as what she used to be. When she came to Christ she was fully convinced that the old Lisa was dead. She is now a new Lisa, and there is no X on her. She can't see why anyone would see himself as damaged goods once Jesus has taken hold of him. She has debunked the myth and refuses to let the culture or the people around her define who she is.

Lisa is rare. Most women I encounter have something in their lives that makes them feel as if there is an X in their collar. (Women will understand that an X in the collar of a blouse indicates that the blouse will sell for less than full price because of being flawed or being leftover in some store's stock!) They have something in their world that tells them they don't measure up. You may have something like that. You may feel you are not smart enough, or pretty enough, or slim enough, or rich enough, or even not spiritual enough. That is the wonderful part about loving and being loved by Jesus. He loves you because He loves you—no matter why you feel you are damaged goods.

OTHER SOURCES OF MYTHS

For some women, the way they were treated as a child has perpetrated a myth in their heads that they are not good enough. One young woman I worked with was the victim of incest by her father. This went on for ten years. She could hardly hold up her head or even speak.

She believed the myth that she was so damaged there was no way she could have a decent life. She clung to that myth because for her it was reality. How on earth could she be of any value if her own father used her and threw her away?

Another woman could never please her mother. Her mother never said much to her, but when she spoke, her words were strong and smothering. Her words defined who the daughter was. Although the daughter is capable and successful, she sees herself as the loser her mother defined. Her mother's words created a mythical belief system to which she still subscribes. She still believes that if your own mother says you will never amount to anything, then you will never amount to anything despite what you accomplish.

A third grade teacher mightily influenced my ability to do math. I know that I am fully capable of understanding advanced concepts. (I passed trigonometry in college.) Mrs. Mason, however, did not like the looks of some of my arithmetic papers. So she held them up in front of the class, my name scrawled across the top of the page, and announced, "This is the kind of paper I never want to see." At that moment, I saw myself as a math-loser. For the rest of my life, I have had to overcome that myth. I read into her disdain for my paper that I was dumb, sloppy, and couldn't "do" math.

She didn't mean that, I hope, but what she said became my reality. "She doesn't like my paper; she thinks my math is flawed; therefore, I am flawed." From that day on, math became an enemy to me. I had never thought about hating it until then. Today I have to work to make peace with my calculator.

Obviously, from the very damaging to the frivolous, if you get the message you are flawed, you will view yourself as flawed. Satan still swishes his sinister tail through peaceful settings, leaving little lies that can grow into mighty myths; concepts held as true because they contain a little truth and a little lie.

- I think of the ministry that paid men more than women because "men have family responsibilities." My question is, "And how about women?" For the same job, is not equal pay the measure of truth?

- I think of the church that won't allow women to have a Bible study during the day. All Bible studies must be in the evening and include men and women so the women won't get ahead of the men spiritually. My question is, "Where is it written?" Since when do we grow in tandem?

- I think of the women's ministry that was led by a man because the women needed "leadership." My question is, "Are women not capable of planning an event for women?"

- I think of the wife who could not have a checking account of her own. Her husband believed that she would be irresponsible, so he said no to her suggestion that she open an account for her own personal expenditures. My question is, "Why is it wrong for a woman to have her own checking account?" I know all of the arguments against it, and I know most of the arguments for it. That is an individual decision, *but* where is it written that it is wrong for a woman to have her own checking account, credit card, or IRA?

I believe the Bible cover to cover, and I believe that God has assigned men and women differing roles and responsibilities in the marriage relationship and in the church. But was it God's intent for women to be viewed as "less than" because their assignments are different? Was it God's plan that women be treated like little children who need attendants? If so, I wonder why He included in the Scripture the stories of such women as Deborah, Abigail, and Esther; or of such women as Naomi, Lydia, Mary, and Priscilla? Why did he include the Proverbs 31 woman, who was fully capable of handling a home, a husband, and business dealings as well? Why was she the "proverbial picture" of the ideal wife? She certainly didn't need a keeper or someone to help her figure out her money.

I am convinced that Satan is the author of the "women are damaged goods" myth that the culture keeps going. He is the one who keeps our heads slightly bent with the nagging thought, "You are 'less than.'"

Many of us have overcome Satan's myths as we have related to great husbands, wonderful friends, supportive pastors, and respectful children. These people in our lives have refused the myth and value us for who we are. But, for others, the myth is still a blinding wet blanket that keeps out the truth. Every day is a question mark. Every day is the wondering, "Do I have value?" When the people around you don't believe you have value, it is an uphill climb to believe the truth in spite of them.

WHEN WE BELIEVE THE MYTH OF DAMAGED GOODS

Unfortunately, when we believe the myth that we are "less than"—that we are damaged goods—there are consequences. No matter how that myth has been played out in your life, whether it has come from gender issues, careless words spoken, or abuse, the results are not pretty. It invariably shows in our behavior.

Preoccupation with Self

It is easy to be preoccupied with yourself when you have gotten the message that you are not valuable or that you are damaged. You don't feel comfortable in your own skin. Each of has the need for someone to care for us. If no one does, then it is very normal for us to become overly invested in trying to feel good about ourselves. That thought may be so far away from your consciousness that you can't explain why you feel the way you do or why you do the things you do. But the truth is, that is the reason we as women sometimes find ourselves obsessed with obtaining things we think we want even though we don't understand why we want them. It is a searching for something to validate who we are or how we look. I see women enhancing their breasts to outrageous proportions to say, "Look at me; I'm a valuable woman. I have bigger breasts than anybody!" What is that but a preoccupation with self to prove a point?

Fortunately, we live in a time when physical abnormalities and deficits can be corrected, and that is a gift of our day much like antibiotics and laser surgery. So I'm not saying that correcting a flaw necessarily represents a preoccupation with surfaces. But when the corrected proportions become greater than life, there is an announcement being made: "I need to be valued and I hope this will do it."

When we become obsessed with anything about our bodies,

whether it is weight, hair, makeup, tans, clothes, or anything else that pertains to the physical side of us, then we know that something else is going on. Somewhere in the back of our minds the myth of damaged goods is lurking. "I am working overtime to prove that the myth is not true. I want to prove that I am not damaged, and I am trying to perfect everything about me to prove it." But there it is, bigger than life!

Lack of Self-Respect

When you fail to respect yourself, many behaviors are dead give-aways. The way you talk about yourself and others is an announcement of how you feel about yourself. The way you allow others to talk to you and treat you is another giveaway. The way you take care of yourself is another. When you believe you don't deserve to be heard or don't deserve to be spoken to with dignity, that reveals that your self-respect is low. Of course, that is not the kind of thing you actually say to yourself: "I don't deserve it." But listen to the people around you. How do they talk to you, and how do you speak with them? Do you hear yourself saying, "I know you don't want to hear this, but . . ."? Do you hear yourself saying, "I know you are going to think I am crazy, but . . ."? Do you demean your message before you even say a word?

How about the way your family speaks to you? I know women whose children speak to them with contempt, yet the mother does nothing about it. If you are like this, you know it is because you fear alienating your children. The faulty notion behind all this makes it so sad, for it is a lack of self-respect that contributes to the alienation. No one respects a person who does not respect herself.

Family and friends will treat you the way you teach them to treat you. If you expect respect and are respectful in return, that sets up an atmosphere for the very thing you want. If you are self-disrespecting, that is what others will give you. When you allow people to believe the myth that you are not worth respectful behavior, they will give you exactly what you expect. You are the one responsible to change others' views of you.

I know it sounds as if you have more power than you really do, but that is the way it works. If you respect yourself, you will be treated with respect. If you are not treated with respect, you should do something about it. If someone treats you disrespectfully, you should treat them well and at the same time explain that you will not stay around for their abusive behavior. "Do unto others as you would have them do unto you" is the principle. Treat the other person with respect but love him enough to stop him from wrong behavior in your presence. That is mutual respect.

Poor Choices

When you believe the myth of damaged goods, you are vulnerable to making poor relational connections. You don't look for people who are good for you, but instead for people who are convenient. You are attracted to people who make you feel good, if only for a moment. Sometimes you will connect to someone who has more money, power, or prestige than you and then live with whatever they may want to give you. You take this behavior, thinking you don't deserve any better. You may connect with someone who has far less than you and who looks at you as his savior. Your effort to pull that individual out of the pit gives you a sense of being valuable. All too often, the effort will leave you dangling. You can't be another's savior, and your effort to pull someone out of a pit will result in your taking the long ride down a slippery slope of dependency, which is one of the major signs of seeing yourself as damaged goods. Both people end up sliding downward. That's just the way it happens.

Dependency Needs

Looking to others to give you a sense of wholeness or allowing others to look to you for their well-being always sets up an entangling dependency. You become dependent on the esteem you have sought in order to feel good about yourself. When that esteem waffles in some way, you are left feeling damaged again—and probably even *more* damaged because you have failed. The mess you are left with is proof to you that you are damaged.

The more situations you get into that are dependency situations, the greater power the myth will have over you. Not only will you see yourself as a needy person, you will also see that you can't meet another's dependency needs—and thereby your feelings of being inadequate and damaged will increase. Never mind that you were not created to meet another's needs for value, nor were they created to meet yours. Things devolve into a Catch-22 situation. Dependencies are a never-ending, unresolvable string of relationships that are not built on decent foundations.

THREE "SELF" WORDS

Three "self" words are easily tangled in the myth of damaged goods: *selfishness, self-esteem,* and *self-respect.* As Christians, we stumble over these words. We aren't exactly sure what to do with them. Various leaders get on "self-esteem" bashing platforms, as if that were a nasty word to be stamped out of the language. Unfortunately, many people misunderstand the importance of our self-view. Some people believe that if you talk about a need for self-esteem in your life, you are weak and self-centered. This view leaves a lot of holes in our understanding of one another. So let's take a look at three "self" words and see if we can clarify what is truth and what is myth.

Selfishness

Selfishness is what God condemns in Scripture. It is sin, and it comes from our natural self. It comes from our flesh, which is always self-protecting and self-absorbed. Selfishness has no marks of goodness in it.

> *Who among you is wise and understanding? Let him show by his good behavior his deeds in the gentleness of wisdom. But if you have bitter jealousy and selfish ambition in your heart, do not be arrogant and so lie against the truth. This wisdom is not that which comes down from above, but is earthly, natural, demonic. For where jealousy and selfish ambition exist, there is disorder and every evil thing. But the wisdom from above is first pure, then peaceable, gentle, reasonable, full of mercy and good fruits, unwavering, without hypocrisy. And the seed whose fruit is righteousness is sown in peace by those who make peace. (JAMES 3:13–18)*

Selfishness tears up peace, spews arrogance, and engages in lies. Selfishness expresses itself in the need for control, the drive to have one's own way, and an " I don't care" attitude when someone else is hurt. Selfishness is never God's way. It is to be shunned and set aside as part of the old way of life.

Self-Esteem

Self-esteem is what we think about ourselves. We cannot give ourselves esteem because that comes from the things we have accomplished. We feel good about ourselves when we do valuable things, have good relationships, have been a good friend, or have excelled in some way (made good grades, baked excellent pies, taught someone how to do a complicated task). There is nothing wrong with feeling good about yourself.

The problem comes when we haven't done enough by our own standard or when someone in our life negates the importance of what we have done. Often our response is to try to do more. Failing that, we sometimes sink into compensating behaviors to keep ourselves buoyed up—behaviors such as disordered eating, overspending, loose moral boundaries, or depression. If we can't achieve a good feeling about ourselves, we may sink into these behaviors to prove that we aren't very valuable. It is easier to prove our lack of value than it is to admit that we might need to change our thinking and maybe even our goals. That is why we can't form our opinion of our value solely on the basis of what we do and what people think of us.

Self-Respect

Self-respect is the goal. To be self-respecting is to see yourself as a woman in whom God has placed immeasurable value and for whom He has planned a future and a hope. Every time you question what the culture says and what other people say about you, stop yourself and say, "Hold it! What is the truth? I am a person of value, and I have a future and a hope!" That is reason to give yourself respect, the respect God has given you!

To respect yourself is to be content with what God has given you and with what He is doing in your life. This is the state Paul describes in Philippians 4:11–13:

> Not that I speak from want, for I have learned to be content in whatever circumstances I am. I know how to get along with humble means, and I also know how to live in prosperity; in any and every circumstance I have learned the secret of being filled and going hungry, both of having abundance and suffering need. I can do all things through Him who strengthens me.

If you have learned how to be content, then you have learned how to be self-sufficient according to the Greek definition of the word. There is a self-sufficiency that relies on God's provision and allows you to have a proper view of yourself, no matter what your outward circumstances. There is a truthful recognition that in yourself you can do nothing, but you can do all things through the strength that has been given to you in Christ (Philippians 4:13). That gift came to you only because God Himself saw fit to come to this earth and die in your place so that you could stand before Him as completed and perfected. You will not stand in your own fleshly (selfish) standard but in the respect that He placed in you, around you, and about you in His Son.

The truth is, we all have Xs in our collars. We are all damaged goods, thanks to our mother Eve's indiscretion in the Garden. But our elder Brother, the Lord and Savior Jesus Christ, has eradicated the X. In the eyes of God, we are not damaged goods. Satan keeps telling us that we are no good and "less than" because we are damaged women. The world wants to pack us into its mold. But Jesus Christ has made us righteous (right with God) and prays continually that we will become the women we are intended to be. "Therefore He is able also to save forever those who draw near to God through Him, since He always lives to make intercession for them" (Hebrews 7:25).

As Jesus Christ prays for us, having set us free from who we were, we will walk circumspectly in the world if we are women who have self-respect. We will be respectful to others as well as to ourselves. We will be able to look at others with kindness and compassion because we aren't seeking anything from people other than pure relationships. We are not needy; therefore, we do not look for someone to meet our dependency needs. They are taken care of because we recognize and relax in the fact that we are well loved. We do not compare ourselves to others because we believe that God has given us what we need and has placed us where we need to be. If He cares this much, how on earth can we keep on acting as if we are "seconds" in a life where first quality gets the esteem?

Like our friend Mary Magdalene, we don't look around us wondering what everyone thinks. We just keep our eyes riveted on Jesus and where He is and what He is doing. That's where we want to be.

THE MYTH
OF
RESPONSIBILITY

I've always wanted to defend her. It just never seemed right that Martha had all the work to do for the care and feeding of Jesus and His men. And when she asks the Master to give her sister Mary a little nudge—well, maybe a big nudge—to help her, Jesus rebukes Martha. Of course, I know that Jesus had His reasons. I trust Him and know He doesn't waste these teachable moments for any of us, but still I feel as if there would have been mighty slim pickings that day if they had waited on Mary to prepare a meal.

I've included the event straight from the Scriptures. Read it and see what you think.

> *Now as they were traveling along, He entered a village; and a woman named Martha welcomed Him into her home. She had a sister called Mary, who was seated at the Lord's feet, listening to His word. But Martha was distracted with all her preparations; and she came up to Him and said, "Lord, do You not care that my sister has left me to do all the serving alone? Then tell her to help me." But the Lord answered and said to her, "Martha, Martha,*

you are worried and bothered about so many things; but only one thing is necessary, for Mary has chosen the good part, which shall not be taken away from her." (LUKE 10:38–42)

Does it seem to you that Martha has a legitimate complaint? She is responsible, and no one is helping her. Who wouldn't feel slighted and frustrated over that? She becomes upset and takes her complaint to the Master. That should have fixed it. Isn't that what we are supposed to do when something goes wrong—take it to Jesus? That's what Martha did, and I am sure she expected that would be the end of the story. Jesus would speak to Mary, and Mary would immediately join Martha in her preparations.

Martha believed a myth and probably didn't know it. Jesus knew it, and for Martha's good it was time to expose the myth for what it was. It was a mixture of truth and lie that was causing His friend Martha great consternation. The Scriptures indicate at first reading that Martha was distressed because she had many preparations to make and no help, especially from Mary, who should have felt the same obligation to prepare food for Jesus and His disciples. It looks as if our sister Martha has a legitimate request and that perhaps our sister Mary is a little too "heavenly minded to be any earthly good."

Jesus, on the other hand, always goes beyond outward appearances and straight to the heart. Because He is total love and total truth, He couldn't go along with Martha in her mythical thinking any more than He can join us in ours. That wouldn't have been healthy and would only have led to more confusion and pain. He had no choice but to speak His healing word of loving rebuke into the conversation.

"Martha, Martha, you are worried and bothered about so many things; but only one thing is necessary, for Mary has chosen the good part, which shall not be taken away from her." Initially, this appears to be really hard on a woman who was just trying to get a meal on the table. But take another look. Everything looked different to me when I saw something that would have been obvious to Martha because she knew the idioms of the language she and Jesus spoke. When we read the account it looks as if it is just the meal that has Martha in a stew. However, there are things which are hidden from our English-speaking minds unless we can catch a glimpse of what Jesus was really saying in the language of the day, *Koine* Greek.

When Jesus said, "Martha, Martha, you are worried and bothered about so many things but only one thing is necessary," Martha would have known that the word for *bothered* is a Greek word for *crowd*. "Martha, Martha, your mind is crowded by so many things, and because of that you can't see what's happening here!"

Jesus went for her heart. He created *a crisis of truth* for Martha. "It looks, My sister, as if you are burdened with cooking, but you are burdened with far more than that. There is a crowd of issues in your mind that is blocking your understanding of what is true and needful in your life. You have a crowd in your mind, and it has to go."

Think of the times your mind has been crowded when something momentous was happening. How many times have you really grasped the import of the moment while it was actually occurring? How often have you wished you could relive the moment just to savor the full import?

Where was your mind when you were saying your wedding vows?

Where was it when you graduated from college?

Where was it when your baby was born?

Where was it when you knew that you had encountered God? Could you fully absorb the moment or were you "bothered with the crowd"?

Martha's crowd had gathered about many things. I cannot begin to imagine all of them, but the fact that she had her adult brother and sister living in her house could have contributed to the crowd. The fact that she and Mary seemed to have extremely differing temperaments probably added some voices to the crowd. The fact that she seemed to be the leader in the family may have brought a crowd member or two. No matter who the members of her crowd were, there is no doubt that the racket created confusion and irritation for our Martha and, as a result, she missed what was really going on! She missed "the better part" and, in His love, Jesus pointed out the real problem.

That was probably very hard for Martha to hear. Put yourself in her shoes for a moment. The Master, your friend, has come to your house. You want to feed Him and make Him comfortable. No one else seems to care that you want to do that. That hurts, and it makes you angry. You decide that you will create your own crisis to get this little situation straightened out because you know that whatever Jesus says, Mary will buy into it. You rush to Jesus, pour your heart out, and He kindly but firmly says, "You are wrong. Mary isn't the problem. You are. In fact, Mary is doing the right thing here."

Imagine the sting! Apart from the sweet healing comfort of the Lord Himself, that kind of thing would have been terribly difficult for a woman like Martha. She was obviously accustomed to being "large and in charge." What she said was "the rule of law" around the kitchen, but on this day she was handed a major paradigm shift. "It is not about your kitchen, Martha. It is not about your responsibility. It is not about what you can do. Martha, Martha, it is about a relationship with Me where eternal words are spoken and heard. It is about kingdom issues that transcend the moment and obliterate your reputation for being a good and gracious hostess. Martha, it is about Me, and Mary has discovered that."

The crowd in her mind had blocked her view. Martha was running on the myth that she was responsible to make something happen that day. It had always been her job to do that, but now she was told, "Your responsibility is to learn of Me. Listen to Me because I have the words of life."

Each of us has "crowds" who seem to be ever-present in our worlds. Finding a way to relate to them without allowing them to take over our minds is the challenge. There is no way to avoid the crowd, but there is a way to live with peace in our lives no matter the situation. That is why understanding the deception in the myth of "I am responsible for the good as well as the bad" is so important.

I AM RESPONSIBLE TO PLEASE EVERYONE

One of the major crowd members is loud and convincing. She likes to keep a conversation going with you that says, "You better be finding out how to please people or you are going to miss out on life." This notion is hard to shake. This myth says that if you aren't in the right place at the right time, saying the right things to the right people, then you are wrecking your chances to succeed. This is a big one in the business world and even in the religious world. You better get out there and talk to the right people about the right things—and whatever you do, don't ruffle any feathers. Don't make anyone mad, don't confront any issues, and you will be all right. The Scriptures do say in Romans 12:18, "As far as it depends on you, be at peace with all men." So it is never our task to stir up trouble. Our goal is peace. But if the price is loss of integrity or perpetrating mythical behavior that only reaps destruction, then it is time to take a second look.

Joyce was a hard-nosed employer who could be very kind to her employees in her small employment agency. She could also be emotionally cruel. People left her employment for that very reason. She was difficult to please and could become abusive when she was displeased. Margaret had started working for Joyce at the beginning—she was her first employee. They had worked hard to get the agency going. They had good days and hard days, but they always seemed to land on their feet with one another.

About five years into the business, Joyce decided that she needed to take a bigger part in the control of the company. Suddenly Margaret, who had been her right-hand person, was left out of meetings and ignored. Thinking that Joyce was just going through a hard time personally, Margaret never questioned what was going on. This separation lasted for three years. Then one day, it was as if it never happened. Margaret was back in favor. She was so relieved to be back "in the know" and helpful to Joyce she didn't recognize that the hatchet was about to fall. The company grew to the point that Joyce needed a manager to take over. She brought in her nephew Nathan straight from the university, and it wasn't long until he called Margaret into his office and told that her services were no longer needed. He offered her a nice one-month package and told her good-bye. Joyce was out of the country, so she was not at the meeting.

Margaret was devastated when she left Nathan's office. For years she had seen herself as helping to hold the company together and working exceptionally hard. Every time things had gone wrong, she had sat with Joyce and tried to reinvent a way to make it all succeed. She had worked overtime to the detriment of herself and her husband John. Now she was gone. A sense of responsibility permeated with the need to please had brought her to this moment. She was without a job. Joyce was aloof and not available even to tell her good-bye. Margaret's years of effort seemed wasted, and at this moment she felt worthless.

The myth of responsibility often leads to this end—when you believe that it is your job to please and take responsibility even though things just don't add up. If you do this long enough, you will find yourself holding a bag of pain. When you do for someone else what she could and should do for herself, you are courting all kinds of "crowd" issues in your mind! You will hear "You're are not working hard enough" shouted out. From the back, the harsh cry of "She doesn't need you anymore. She never did need you!" Then when you are no longer viable in the relationship, it will dawn on you that all of this responsibility and people pleasing is your issue, not the other person's.

The crowd in your mind tries to convince you that you could do more, be more, and try more to gain approval, acceptance, and gratitude. The truth, however, is that you had expectations of a payoff from assuming a responsibility that wasn't yours. You expected a response for the pleasing you were doing. When you didn't get it, the crowd reminded you that you had worked so hard—and what good had it done for you? You set yourself up to feel pain, and sure enough it really hurts.

In some ways this myth relates to the myth of damaged goods, but this one is even more specific. It has to do with a general feeling toward the world. "I can't upset anyone because that would be wrong." "I can't draw boundaries because that would be cruel." "I can't express my preferences because that would be selfish." These thoughts float like clouds across the sky of your mind and become thunderheads when you are confronted with a situation in which you are challenged to respond.

The Bible does not say so, but I wonder if Martha struggled with this need to please everyone, and so, like many of us, ended up missing what was really happening in her home that day. I wonder if she would have liked to sit and listen to her friend Jesus, but because she had the need to please everyone, she just couldn't let herself do it. She would have felt terrible if anyone had thought that she was lazy, a poor hostess, or heaven forbid, as unaware as her sister, Mary, who seemed to have her head in the clouds. Instead of coming to Jesus and saying, "Lord, I would love to sit here and listen to you, but I just don't feel right about it. It seems too irresponsible when there is so much work to do"; instead of dealing with the Lord about her own issues, Martha attacked Mary and demanded that Jesus make Mary be just like her. She believed the myth that the only way she could be an all right person was to make sure everyone was pleased—and she assumed that they would be pleased only if they were cared for as she cared for everyone.

In Martha's mind, a meal was not a meal if you didn't work up a sweat over it. Translated into today's language, "If you don't make it from scratch, you aren't really cooking." If you simply bought a loaf of bread at the bakery and brought it home, everyone would be so disappointed. Never mind that you might have time to sit and have a cup of coffee with your family, or to work a puzzle with your son, or to take a walk with your granddaughter, or to not be too tired to actually enjoy going to bed with your husband!

I AM RESPONSIBLE TO MAKE IT WORK

Emily believed the myth that she was responsible to please her boyfriend, Robert, no matter what. If she failed to do so, that would be the end of the relationship. She had picked up that myth somewhere in her childhood when she saw her mother pretend about so many things. She pretended to listen to Emily's father while he went on and on about his golf game. She pretended to enjoy sitting in the living room while her husband flipped the TV channels with the remote. She pretended to enjoy watching baseball games with him. He never spoke to her other than to ask her to get him something to drink or eat. He wasn't mean—he was disconnected.

Emily saw her mother scurry to keep him happy, or at least to keep him from complaining. She grew up believing that if you wanted to keep a man, you were responsible to do whatever would keep peace with him no matter what that was. Her father never said much, but it seemed to Emily that her mother pretended to find him fascinating and interesting just to make him happy. Not much integrity in that, but it worked for Mom and Dad. At least they were still married.

When Emily went away to a Christian college, she met Robert. He was handsome and popular, and she was thrilled that he had taken notice of her. Robert had some very heady ideas he demanded of Emily. If she wanted to be his girlfriend, then she would need to let her hair grow and wear no makeup. She would need to be very careful about the clothes she wore. He would not tolerate any clothing he interpreted as being too revealing. Consequently, on more than one occasion, he sent her back to her room to change her blouse. She disliked the feeling his demands gave her, but she felt within her heart that to have a godly boyfriend, she needed to do whatever it took to keep him. It was her responsibility.

Since Robert did not demand that she have sex with him—in fact, he avoided even holding her hand—Emily convinced herself that the least she could do was go along with such a fine, moral man. The only problem was that by assuming responsibility for the relationship, she was losing zeal for . . . life. She had handed the control of her well-being to Robert because she believed she was responsible to do whatever was moral to keep him happy.

Of course, the truth is that her efforts did not keep him happy—they only gave him a platform to exalt his own power. When he wearied of her "Yes your majesty, no your majesty" demeanor, he decided that God wanted him to look elsewhere for a life mate. Emily was brokenhearted. She could not believe that neither Robert nor God was honoring her peace-at-any-price responsibility! Similarly, Martha was probably shocked when Jesus said, "Martha, Martha, . . . Mary has chosen the better part!"

In each of our lives, it is a stretch to recognize that we are responsible only for our own behavior and the repercussions in our own lives. When we wander into that nebulous fantasyland of "I am responsible for the good as well as the bad," we step into a quagmire of confusion.

ANXIETY IS THE PAYOFF

If you have been caught up in the I-am-responsible myth, then you inevitably will have the emotional payoff of anxiety. Your focus of necessity is locked into what is happening around you because, after all, you are responsible to make good things happen and avoid making bad things happen. Like Martha, your eyes are on the vegetables in the stew pot—not on the Creator of the vegetables, who is sitting in your living room waiting to give you the "better part."

Your focus causes the anxiety. It doesn't change the situation, but it causes you to feel the full burden of whatever happens. Your mind constantly swirls with questions. If you are responsible for a meal, your mind screams, "Will there be enough? Will the food taste good? Will there be more tomorrow if I need it? Do people want something in addition to what I have here? Do people want it prepared another way? What can I do to make the pot look more appealing?"

And on and on it goes. When anxiety hits, it covers a lot of territory. You become the source and the resource for everyone, and if you are not enough, no one is happy. You are not experiencing the life you were intended to live and, amazingly, as long as you assume the responsibility, neither is anyone else!

ABUNDANT LIFE

At one point in His ministry, Jesus spoke about the people who come to Him, and He compared them to sheep. He spoke of Himself as the Good Shepherd who watched over the sheep who were His. Then He made this statement about Satan, who always seems to be around when there is pain, misery, and destruction: "The thief comes only to steal and kill and destroy; I came that they may have life, and have it abundantly" (John 10:10). (Remember what Satan wants you to believe about God? *He doesn't mean what He says, and He is holding out on you.*)

Sheep have a remarkable ability to hold on to an idea when the reason for it has vanished. Ken Johnson talks, for example, about a sheep's unthinking interest in following the crowd. It never asks, "Why am I doing this?"

> One chilly morning . . . after showering and shaving, I slid into my coveralls and headed for the barn to tend to the sheep. As I opened the barn door and called to them, I grabbed a hoe to do a quick cleanup just outside the door. I could hear the sleepy sheep moving about, beginning to shuffle toward the doorway.
>
> Acting on a playful impulse, I took the hoe handle and held it in front of the first ewe, about knee high, as she started out the door. Instead of stopping, she gracefully leaped over the stick and proceeded, without hesitation, toward the pasture.

I pulled the hoe handle away, but was fascinated to see what happened next. One after another, each of the remaining twenty sheep came to where the first ewe had jumped—and duplicated the feat! As if on command, each sheep launched itself into the air at that precise spot, completed its jump, and then fell in step with the animal directly in front of it.

What a curious sight! The fact that the original reason for jumping—the hoe handle—had been taken away did not seem to concern the little flock of sheep at all. All they knew was that the sheep immediately in front had jumped, and that seemed to be reason enough for doing the same. . . .

As I think about it, I am amazed how much we are like those little lambs in our daily activities. Many of our revered, established traditions today continue long after their original reasons have ceased to exist.[1]

When it comes to the things that you have believed you are ultimately responsible to make happen, Satan has a grand time making you miserable and making you jump, even when that approach has failed you many times and never was valid. He will hit you with anxious thoughts: "If you had done more, this would not have happened." "If you don't worry about it, they won't think you love them." Or maybe even the subtle lie, "If you just disappeared from the picture, everyone would be better off." There are many ways that anxiety can creep into the picture and rob you of your joy, kill your spirit, and destroy your desire to go on! Isn't that an obvious work of the Enemy?

Doesn't the myth become clear when you see the results in your life? If you are unable to have joy and peace while holding on to the myth, something is wrong. The part that is not true is causing problems, and the more you hold on to it, the more the problems escalate. Whatever God says we are to do, works. Whatever He says is good for us brings wholeness and health. But when we jump in and believe a lie, we get caught in the web of anxiety.

Look at what Jesus said about worry and anxiety in Matthew 6:24–34:

"No one can serve two masters; for either he will hate the one and love the other, or he will be devoted to one and despise the other. You cannot

serve God and wealth. [That which enables you to get what you want!]

"For this reason I say to you, do not be worried about your life, as to what you will eat or what you will drink; nor for your body, as to what you will put on. Is not life more than food, and the body more than clothing? Look at the birds of the air, that they do not sow, nor reap nor gather into barns, and yet your heavenly Father feeds them. Are you not worth much more than they? And who of you by being worried can add a single hour to his life? And why are you worried about clothing? Observe how the lilies of the field grow; they do not toil nor do they spin, yet I say to you that not even Solomon in all his glory clothed himself like one of these. But if God so clothes the grass of the field, which is alive today and tomorrow is thrown into the furnace, will He not much more clothe you? You of little faith! Do not worry then, saying, 'What will we eat?' or 'What will we drink?' or 'What will we wear for clothing?' For the Gentiles eagerly seek all these things; for your heavenly Father knows that you need all these things. But seek first His kingdom and His righteousness, and all these things will be added to you.

"So do not worry about tomorrow; for tomorrow will care for itself. Each day has enough trouble of its own."

When you read those words, they sound comforting, but your heart cries out, " Oh, dear Lord, how on earth am I going to give up worrying when I care so much?" Is that not the question? When the need is obvious and your care is great, you believe there just has to be something you should be doing. When that thought grips your heart, anxiety has you. Can you see how the old myths from the Garden creep in on you? God's holding out on you, and God doesn't mean what He says. So someone better be in charge of worrying here. Someone has to feel the anxiety.

Reread Matthew 6:24–34 and ask yourself the following questions. (Sometimes we just have to take hold of our minds and get some reasoning done!)

1. Who is in control?

2. Who will take care of you: your resources (what you can come up with) or the God who takes care of the birds? Several years ago we had a blizzard, and for four days not one sound of a bird was heard.

They were totally silent. But as the snow began to melt and the sun came out, amazingly so did the birds. The weather had been brutal, and I had not seen or heard a single bird in four days.

On that fourth afternoon when the chirping began again, I could not help noticing that I didn't see one dead bird. They didn't freeze to death, or starve, or die of thirst. God had taken care of them, and I didn't even see Him do it. I just saw the result; there were fat, healthy birds singing with all their might. They couldn't help themselves—only God could be responsible for them!

3. Does God know your need? Does He know the burden you are carrying?

4. What can you do about tomorrow or anything that will happen tomorrow that might cause you distress?

When you have answered the questions, look back and see what you *can* do. It is miserable not to be able to do anything when you believe that you are responsible for whatever happens, whether it is good or bad. God knows we need to do something. We just need to know what to do. The words of Jesus in Matthew 6:33 in *The Amplified Bible* read like this: "But seek for (aim at and strive after) first of all His kingdom and His righteousness [His way of doing and being right], and then all these things taken together will be given to you besides."

This was Christ's message to Martha. "Martha, Martha, Mary is aiming at and striving at My way of doing and being right.

"It isn't your way, Martha, but it is My way. It is the better part."

Satan's dialogue in all of this will be subtle and suggestive. "How can you live with yourself and not be more involved?" The old myth-maker himself will chew away at your peace and joy. As you look at the circumstances and wring your hands about what you should be doing, or even as you barge in and take charge, inevitably you have to look at the result. Is what you are doing working? Do you have peace and are you closer to the Lord now than before you jumped in and assumed what you believed to be your responsibility?

First Peter 5:6–9 is a great Scripture passage.

> *Therefore humble yourselves under the mighty hand of God, that He may exalt you at the proper time, casting all your anxiety on Him, because He cares for you. Be of sober spirit, be on the alert. Your adversary, the devil, prowls around like a roaring lion, seeking someone to devour. But resist him, firm in your faith, knowing that the same experiences of suffering are being accomplished by your brethren who are in the world.*

When you decide that you want to "seek first the kingdom of God and His righteousness," you are making the choice to humble yourself under the mighty hand of God. That means that you are willing to let Him be in charge. You are open to His results being the final outcome.

Can you think of an area of your life where you have worked overtime being responsible? Is there a person or a situation that the crowd in your mind calls out to you about all the time? Have you wanted to have your way, to have things work out the way you wanted them to, the way that you had planned?

You see, Satan wants his way, and he wants to trap others into entangling themselves in the no-win pursuit of their own way. He is doomed already for his actions in the Garden, but if he can devour you, he will. He will use any way he can to confuse people and convince those who seek God that maybe God won't come through, that He holds out on people, that He doesn't mean what He says. So we take the "bull by the horns" and jump in to make things work. We believe that we are responsible and we rush in to make a bigger mess than the mess we have seen.

A story from the Internet about a man named Charles Chu tells a tale all of us overly zealous responsibility-myth-believers can relate to:

> A few years ago I had a chance to become a hero, but it turned out to be an embarrassing moment. I was in China on a tour group. Our tour bus was on the way to a scenic spot with another tour bus in front of us. It was snowing, and the road was muddy. Suddenly the bus ahead of us skidded off the road and tipped over on its side in a rice field. I quickly jumped off my tour bus, ran to the overturned bus, and jumped on

top. Windows were shattered, and people inside were obviously hurt. The emergency door was facing upward, so I grabbed the handle of the emergency door and pulled. The door did not open. I kept pulling hard, but it wouldn't budge. By this time, others had come and were pulling people out through the windows, so I gave up on the door and joined them. After I moved away from the door, another man went over to the door. He turned the door handle, and the door opened easily. I suddenly realized why the door did not open for me: I had been standing on the door as I tried to open it. With good intentions to save lives, I had become the biggest obstacle blocking the door of rescue.

In her book *The Christian's Secret of a Happy Life,* Hannah Whitall Smith writes these words about the Lord's carrying our burdens and managing our affairs. They are worthy of some major meditation time. So chew slowly!

In laying off your burdens, therefore, the first one you must get rid of is yourself. You must hand yourself, with your temptations, your temperament, your frames and circumstances, feelings, and all your inward and outward experiences, over into the care of your God, and leave it all there. He made you, and therefore He understands you, and knows how to manage you; and you must trust Him to do it. Say to Him, "Here, Lord, I abandon myself to thee. I have tried in every way I could think of to manage myself, and to make myself what I know I ought to be, but have always failed. Now I give it up to thee. Do thou take entire possession of me. Work in me all the good pleasure of thy will. Mold and fashion me into such a vessal as seemeth good to thee. I leave myself in thy hands, and I believe that thou wilt, according to thy promise, and make me into a vessel unto thy own honor, 'sanctified, and meet for the master's use, and prepared unto every good work.'" And here you must rest, trusting yourself thus to Him, continually and absolutely.[2]

When it finally dawns on us that we cannot even handle ourselves apart from God's overruling power, it certainly puts a different perspective on the I-am-responsible myth.

THAT OTHER THING I AM RESPONSIBLE FOR

There is another side of the myth that is powerful. If you believe it is yours to make things happen, then you have believed the side of the myth that says, "You've got the power!" Just think about it. If you can build it, fix it, or rearrange it, then you are a pretty powerful person. The payoff is a tenuous peace at any price! That makes you feel good because you are responsible to make sure everyone is OK. If it looks good, then you feel good. At least you feel good until you realize the price you pay for that peace. It may be the loss of self-respect, compromised integrity, or an ongoing sense of distance from God— but you have pulled off peace, and that feels good. But when things are ruffled, anxiety sets in and you are immediately kicked into the "I have to make things happen here" mode.

The really condemning, power-sapping side of the myth is found when you believe that you are responsible for whatever bad that happens. You know for sure that you have no power to make things better in your world or in anyone else's, but you *really* believe you are responsible for things that go wrong. Satan, that old liar, has deceived you into believing that because of some flaw in your character or because of some past indiscretion, you are the problem in every situation in which you find yourself.

I have a good friend who was raised in a very negative home. It was so negative that she planned to leave home when she graduated from high school and never come back. She made those plans when she was a second grader, and she was true to her plan. She never went home again. The problem was, she left home with the legacy of a myth—a myth that said, "If you have anything to do with any situation, you will fail and cause others to fail."

My friend went so far as to refuse to cheer for a popular baseball team because she thought that if she wanted them to win, they were doomed to fail. You can see, of course, that Satan's tail had swished through her mind and left a deep rut. It was a lie that was absorbed into the myth she clung to. She controlled the effect of the myth by staying aloof from any situation where she might cause a problem. Gratefully, she now has taken charge of the myth and replaced it with the truth, but the myth had enormous power over her for many years. If she lets her guard down, it is still easy for her to believe she caused the difficulty, no matter what it was.

Do you ever feel that whatever you touch will be damaged?

Do you feel absolutely powerless to do anything constructive?

You may feel that way because of someone's words toward you—or because of someone's actions, or because experience has taught you, "Don't plan on having a good impact here." If any of that is true of you, you have a crowd in your mind that causes you stress that binds you.

In his book *You Can Be Happy No Matter What,* Richard Carlson makes an interesting observation about stress. I believe it is part of the means of silencing and eliminating the crowd in your mind.

> Surprisingly, the solution to stress is to begin to lower your tolerance to stress. This is the opposite of what most of us have been taught, but it is the truth. Lowering your tolerance for stress is based on the simple principle that our level of stress will always be exactly equal to our current tolerance. This is why people who can handle lots of stress always have to do just that. . . .
>
> The lower our tolerance for stress, the better off we are psychologically. When our goal is to feel our stress as early as possible, we can "nip stress in the bud" earlier, and return to a more positive state. We have choices; in fact, we have a series of "choice points" in any situation. The longer we wait to disregard the stressful thoughts, the more difficult it becomes to bring ourselves back to our natural state of mind. Eventually, with practice, any of us can get to the point where we are aware of our negative thoughts before they pull us off track. Remember, you are just one thought away from a nice feeling.
>
> This new way of understanding stress is not a prescription for laziness or apathy . . . in fact, it's the opposite. The more peaceful and happy we feel inside, the less distracted we are by our own thinking, the more productive and effective we can be in all areas of our lives.[3]

This is a psychological explanation of the wonderful words of Paul in Philippians 4:6–9:

> *Be anxious for nothing, but in everything by prayer and supplication with thanksgiving let your requests be made known to God. And the peace*

of God, which surpasses all comprehension, will guard your hearts and your minds in Christ Jesus.

Finally, brethren, whatever is true, whatever is honorable, whatever is right, whatever is pure, whatever is lovely, whatever is of good repute, if there is any excellence and if anything worthy of praise, dwell on these things. The things you have learned and received and heard and seen in me, practice these things, and the God of peace will be with you.

Don't lie to yourself and say, "I am so stressed because I have this great responsibility." If you believe that, you will live in stress and establish a pattern that will be destructive to yourself and others. Have you ever heard yourself repeatedly cite a litany of burdens? Maybe the holidays bring your litany to the forefront. "Oh, I hate the holidays. They are always so much work. We have gotten into a habit of spending too much, eating too much, and just overdoing." Next year, same litany. What is that but stress, anxiety, and worry coming out on a regular basis? Maybe it is your weight. Some of us have an ongoing internal and external dialogue going on. "I have to lose weight. I know I have to lose weight." Every bite we put into our mouths produces anxiety, stress, and worry.

If God says, "Be anxious for nothing," He means, "Be anxious for *nothing.*" When you believe the I-am-responsible myth and believe that God is holding out on you, and believe that God doesn't mean what He says, you are inviting anxiety, stress, and worry to find a home within you. Ultimately, you will begin to see your mind, soul, and body affected. You will ask yourself, "How did I get into this shape?" And, as we know, you reach this condition one day at a time as you nod and say, "I know, I know" to truth and go right on doing what you have always done. Don't ever forget the oh, so true definition of insanity—doing the same things in the same way and expecting different results.

Remember, Jesus came that we might have life and have it abundantly. In order to experience that abundance in fullness, the crowd in our mind has to go. One by one, we have to run the squatters out. They will try to sneak back in, but the minute you begin to sense the whining voice of one of the crowd trying to distract you, it is up to you to take charge and refuse the urges that they are so good at producing.

The crowd is under your control. Your job is to recognize that you have a crowd. Identify who they are. Run them out of your mind. Slam the door, and keep them out. No one can do this for you. If you want the peace that passes understanding that Jesus promises to all who belong to Him, the crowd has to go.

> *The question to ask at the end of life's race is not so much "What have I accomplished?" but "Whom have I loved, and how courageously?"*
>
> —Geoff Gorsuch, "Journey to Adelphos,"
> *Discipleship Journal*[4]

CHAPTER FIVE

THE MYTH
OF
MARRIAGE IS
THE ANSWER

When we make anything or anyone "the answer" in our lives, we have missed it.

Many people who are in marriages are missing it. They believed a myth when they signed on for holy matrimony, and they continue to believe that myth despite the overwhelming evidence that marriage is not the answer to life's problems. Consequently, they are disappointed and wondering what on earth is going on.

You may be one of those people who believed that you were marrying your other half. You were joining with the person who was going to complete your world and bring sunshine to your cloudy days. You were going to run through the meadow of life, and your mate would always be waiting to catch you and welcome you with open arms. If you believed anything like that, and if what you expected hasn't happened, I guarantee that you are hurt and wondering why you are unhappy!

It is a myth that union with another person makes you a whole, peaceful, content, and joyful person. No person can offer that in your life.

A pastor told the following story in a recent sermon, and he hit the point squarely on the head.

> A man told me he had been dating a woman for several years, and she was starting to wonder if they would ever marry. He told me he didn't know if he could marry her because, as he said to me, "I don't think she makes me happy."
>
> I asked him why not, which was a mistake. He went on and on explaining all the reasons why she didn't make him happy.
>
> Finally I interrupted and asked, "What kind of wife would make you happy?" The more he described what he was looking for in a wife, the more convinced I became that what he really needed was not a wife. He needed a goldfish, the pretty kind with the long tail that floats around, or maybe a Golden Retriever—but even a dog will make demands on you emotionally. A goldfish, though, just sits there and looks pretty and doesn't ask you to communicate. It doesn't ask you how your day was or expect you to listen to how its day was. The last thing he needed was a wife, because his whole understanding of why the world existed was to meet his needs.[1]

A wife or husband will not meet your needs.

A good marriage is a rare and wonderful thing to be nourished and cherished, but it cannot supply the security and stability for which we all long. What if something happens to alter things? What if someone changes? What if illness or death intervenes? What if unseen emotional problems crop up? There has to be more to life than having a wonderful marriage. If a good marriage is all you need to be happy and fulfilled in life and you are not married, then you have been cheated.

- A precious young couple I love is going through enormous struggle right now. Eleven weeks into their marriage, they discovered that the young husband had a terminal brain tumor. Over the past four years they have fought a valiant battle to save his life, but at this point they are losing. He is deteriorating day by day. If marriage is the answer to the pains and problems of life, Greg and Michelle have missed it. Neither their love nor their commitment to have a godly marriage has given them any peace. It has only thrown them into an arena where they have been tested at every turn.

• Julie is a wonderful woman who has prayed for a mate for years. She has faithfully served God, and yet the desire of her heart has gone unmet. She is single at the age of fifty, and while she is not unhappy, she does not feel complete. She longs for a mate, prays for a mate, and subliminally believes that somehow she could relax if only she had a mate.

• Carol and Joe are middle-aged and struggling. They always have struggled. They married too early, had too many children, and life has thrown them too many challenges. At least, that's what they think. Carol blames Joe for what he hasn't done for her, and Joe blames Carol for what is wrong. They both blame the marriage for their misery.

The truth is that each of them is creating his personal misery as he holds on to the belief that if the marriage were OK each of them could be just fine. They both believe that everything would be fine if the other fulfilled his side of the marriage. That sounds good, but the problem with that kind of thinking is that this makes Joe's behavior responsible for Carol's well-being and Carol's behavior responsible for Joe's.

So it is obvious that marriage is not the answer to all of our ills. Marriage is a unique and wonderful relationship, but it cannot heal your emotions and make you whole.

MARRIAGE MYTHS

Marriage myths that waft through the air hit different generations in interesting ways. Any little doubt the Enemy whispers in the ear will shatter peace and create the confusion and strife he loves. He has a different suggestion for each generation. That myth then invades the culture and women find themselves in bondage and misery.

In the sixties, when I was engaged and looking forward to marriage, my greatest concern was to pick out silver that complemented the china I had chosen. Looking back, I think, "Where was my head?" Society, marriage magazines, and my contemporaries formed my thoughts. It was a time when many of us believed that if we married, we had achieved the ultimate goal. If we had the right silver and china, we could create a home. If we married, we would be normal and have a normal home. (Never mind that we didn't know what that meant, but we thought we knew the way to get "it.") Normal women were engaged and married in their early twenties. Abnormal women were not. That was the thought that filtered through our generation. Consequently, one would have been foolish to pass up an opportunity to marry!

I took the opportunity (normal, remember?) and I don't regret it, but I did think that when we met at the altar everything would be wonderful. It never occurred to me that this man and I would have adjustments to make. The fact that we would grow and change was nowhere on my radar screen. I was clueless to the fact that our marriage would be sorely tested by the same things everyone experiences. I thought we were different. I naively believed that our love would keep us from facing anything that could trouble us.

Well, our marriage has endured in spite of what I believed, certainly not because of it! We did something at the beginning that has made a difference. We both meant it when we agreed that we would stick together no matter what. That commitment has made the rough places passable. At times we have hobbled instead of run, but by God's grace we are moving on.

In those first rocky years, I was shocked that we were different, that we thought differently, and that there were times when we didn't like each other. I couldn't believe it, but since marriage was what normal people did and because I was committed, I decided that I would stick it out through thick or thin. It took several years for me to give up the myth that my husband would make the cloudy days sunny and would be waiting at the other end of the meadow for me when I ran into his arms. I finally decided that I would enjoy the cloudy days and give up running through meadows. That made our relationship far more authentic.

During that era, my mythical kind of thinking was common. The norm was to jump into the roller coaster called marital bliss, strap yourself in, and believe it would all be wonderful—after all, it was *nor-*

mal! If it turned out not to be, well, you just endured or, if necessary, you divorced. No one planned for such an eventuality, but if it happened, that was the answer for problems. Some couples didn't divorce but struggled along in silent bitterness. They lived like caged animals enduring until the end. The whole marriage thing was supposed to secure the completion we longed for, but my generation can testify that is a myth. So there has to be something beyond the myth that marriage makes everything wonderful because, let's face it, it doesn't.

In the last twenty-five years, there has been a cultural flip-flop. The old myth that didn't pan out to be true has been replaced with another myth that breeds equal misery and confusion. Today many believe that marriage will ruin everything—so let's just live together and see if we can make it work *before* we make the commitment. In fact, "Why should we make a legal commitment? We love one another. Isn't that enough before God?"

At either end of the mythological scale from, "Let's get married no matter what" to "Let's don't get married and ruin a good thing," the couple and their relationship still are not the focus. One extreme deifies marriage while the other strips it of its sacred qualities. Both are based on mythical beliefs that create misery. Marriage is viewed as something to be desired on the one hand and avoided on the other. Some believe marriage is what normal people do. Others ask, "What's so normal about marriage?" To avoid the confusion and pain of either end of the scale, it is important to see what God says marriage is and what He says marriage is not.

Remember, there is a liar whose name is Satan, and he is hanging around to keep you confused. *As in the other myths, he wants to make you think that God is holding out on you and that He doesn't mean what He says.* What better place for him to swish his arrogant tail than right through the tender union of marriage?

⊹

MARRIAGE VERSUS COHABITATION
The Deceiver's Playground

The number of "unmarried-couple households" has increased from 523,000 in 1970 to 4,236,000 in 1998. Professor Roger Rubin, a University of Maryland specialist in family studies, says, "We estimate that by the year 2000, half of all American adults will have had a cohabiting experience by the age of 30."

Fact #1: The *Houston Chronicle* reports that couples who live together have an 80 percent greater chance of divorce than those who don't cohabit.

Fact #2: A Washington State researcher discovered that women who cohabit are twice as likely to experience domestic violence as married women. The National Center for Mental Health revealed that cohabiting women's incidence of depression is four times greater than that of married women, and two times greater than unmarried women.

Fact #3: In a survey of over 100 couples who lived together, 71 percent of the women said they would not live-in again.

"Three Facts" from Christian Single *(September 1999), 29.*

⊹

Let's take a look together at God's first words about marriage. (Remember the principle of first mention when you read the Bible. Wherever something is mentioned in Scripture for the first time, that meaning follows it through the Scriptures.)

Then the LORD God said, "It is not good for the man to be alone; I will make him a helper suitable for him." Out of the ground the LORD God formed every beast of the field and every bird of the sky, and brought them to the man to see what he would call them; and whatever the man called a living creature, that was its name. The man gave names to all the cattle, and to the birds of the sky, and to every beast of the field, but for Adam there was not found a helper suitable for him. So the LORD *God caused a deep sleep to fall upon the man, and he slept; then He took one of his ribs and closed up the flesh at that place. The* LORD *God fashioned into a woman the rib which He had taken from the man, and brought her to the man. The man said,*

"This is now bone of my bones,
And flesh of my flesh;
She shall be called Woman,
Because she was taken out of Man."

For this reason a man shall leave his father and his mother, and be joined to his wife; and they shall become one flesh. And the man and his wife were both naked and were not ashamed. (GENESIS 2:18–25)

There you have it. This is God's first mention of marriage. Because the woman was taken from Adam, they had a special relationship. It was a very important relationship that drew the couple straight toward one another. "For this reason, a man shall leave his father and mother, and be joined to his wife; and they shall become one flesh." One man and one woman were to be joined together for a lifetime. The unique mark of their relationship was to be sexual intercourse (one flesh). That was what set apart marriage from every other relationship. That was God's intent. Sexual intercourse was a mark, a sign, and a privilege of the marriage agreement. That is why sexual intercourse with anyone but your marital partner is so serious and ultimately so deadly.

Take a minute and read this story of the Pharisee's encounter with Jesus as it is recorded in the gospel of Matthew:

Some Pharisees came to Jesus, testing Him and asking, "Is it lawful for a man to divorce his wife for any reason at all?" And He answered and said, "Have you not read that He who created them from the beginning made them male and female, and said, 'For this reason a man shall leave his father and mother and be joined to his wife, and the two shall become one flesh'? So they are no longer two, but one flesh. What therefore God has joined together, let no man separate." (MATTHEW 19:3–6)

Jesus was making the point that the two who were different (but whole) were to come together sexually, and when they did, they were *one flesh*. He went on to explain that one thing could divide a marriage. That one thing was when the "one flesh" part of the agreement was violated.

Step back into the shadows and pretend that you are listening to this interchange—it is profound:

> *They said to Him, "Why then did Moses command to give her a certificate of divorce and send her away?" He said to them, "Because of your hardness of heart Moses permitted you to divorce your wives; but from the beginning it has not been this way. "And I say to you, whoever divorces his wife, except for immorality, and marries another woman commits adultery."* (MATTHEW 19:7–9, EMPHASIS ADDED)

This discussion of the heart of marriage is more important than what we see at first glance. Think about your own perception of marriage and ask yourself, "Have I believed something different from what Jesus said?" He repeated the words from Genesis that to have a marriage it took a male and a female willing to leave home, stick to one another like glue, and have sexual intercourse. The two become one flesh, but they are still two people. The thing that could tear up the marriage was not the differences of the genders or the things on which they disagreed, but whether they defiled the marriage bed and joined their body with another. That could leave a marriage covenant shattered. The tearing of "one flesh" was the thing that could release a partner from his or her promise to leave and cleave. It wasn't commanded, but it was allowed.

What does that have to do with anything? Well, think of this. How many different versions of how to have a happy marriage have you heard of? How many formulas, models, how-to's, and sermons about marriage have you heard? How many have you been able to implement in your own life?

I believe the first mention of marriage was simple because it had to be. We women are all different from one another and the men we marry are all different from one another. For the many different combinations of couples that would come together, there would be an equal number of ways to live out the marriage. If leaving Mom and Dad behind was achieved, if the sticking together was accomplished, and if intercourse was maintained, then you had marriage.

I think we have complicated the issue and layered over our understanding of what God wants us to know about marriage by creating formulas and models and encouraging couples to fit into them. If they don't fit the models, they become dissatisfied with their marriages. They don't measure up.

I think this is particularly true for women. We are relational, and we like to fit in. If we don't have the kind of marriage that is described as ideal, or if we are disappointed when our husband doesn't fit into the mold of the godly husband, it is hard for us to accept.

Yet it breeds dissatisfaction to focus on what you don't have. It would be more constructive to look at what you *do* have. Have you left your home of origin, are you sticking with one another, and are you sleeping with one another? Then you have God's plan for marriage. From that point you can grow myriad ways, but the basics are there for the relationship to last.

Years ago I attended a morning worship service at a small church. It was small enough that the pastor had time to walk among the congregation and greet everyone. When he reached the pew where an elderly woman was sitting alone, he greeted her warmly and asked her where Henry was. "Home in the bed, I guess," she said with a matter-of-factness that surprised my young mind. I couldn't believe that she would just say what her husband was doing without trying to sugarcoat it. She wasn't being bitter or disrespectful—she was speaking the truth and letting her husband be responsible for himself.

Because we have believed the myth that marriage means we are one individual rather than two people who have left our homes of origin, committed ourselves to one another, and have monogamous sexual intercourse, we make some huge mistakes.

It is my observation that this is why we women struggle with letting our husbands be who they are. It is the thing that keeps us from speaking the truth about our relationship. If we encounter problems, we don't want to face them because that would mean we don't fit into the mold.

I have smiled many times as I listened to some of the popular teachings on marriage because, although I've been married over thirty-five years, for the life of me, I have never been able to make my marriage fit into the mold! We have always been able to fit into God's simple, three-point Genesis design, but so many other templates have left us as misfits. Do you ever feel that way? Early on, the fact that we didn't fit the pattern was troubling to me. I tried to change my husband to fit the mold, and I tried to twist myself into what I was hearing, but I just couldn't do it. When I finally gave up trying to force our relationship to conform to the Christian seminar model of marriage, voilá, we were both happier.

What I had to learn was to ask the question, "Where is it written?" Some of the ideas that have floated through Christendom over the past couple of decades have sounded wonderful. If you take them at face value, they might be interesting and perhaps even provocative. But if you stopped to ask, "Where is it written?" you might have been surprised.

Out of respect for my fellow Christians who sincerely believe they are right, I don't want to name any particular teachings, but I do want to give you a tool you can use whenever anything seems not to fit. *Trust your instincts.* If something doesn't seem to fit, ask the question, "Where is it written?" and then proceed to ask God the Holy Spirit to guide you! He was sent to this earth to accomplish several specific tasks. One of the most specific and significant was to guide us "into all truth!" (John 16:13).

WHAT ABOUT SINGLENESS?

Marriage is important, but it is not the holy temple everyone must visit in order to have a meaningful relationship with Christ or a blessed and fulfilling life. In that same discussion when Jesus answered the Pharisees' questions about divorce He answered His disciples' question about marriage like this:

> *The disciples said to Him, "If the relationship of the man with his wife is like this, it is better not to marry." But He said to them, "Not all men can accept this statement, but only those to whom it has been given. For there are eunuchs who were born that way from their mother's womb; and there are eunuchs who were made eunuchs by men; and there are also eunuchs*

who made themselves eunuchs for the sake of the kingdom of heaven. He who is able to accept this, let him accept it." (MATTHEW 19:10–12)

Even Jesus Himself said that not everyone had to be married. Some people are given the gift of singleness. (A eunuch in biblical times was someone who had been castrated, but the principle that carries over today is to define a eunuch as someone who is not sexually active and thus not married.) For those who are given the gift of singleness, for those who were born that way, for those who were made that way by others, or for those who have made that choice themselves, Jesus Himself says to accept it.

Since that is the case, it would never make good sense that what married people are given is some sort of completeness and life-joy that is withheld from single people. Married people are not handed the key to bliss while single people are left standing behind the proverbial door! Obviously, there is another relationship that is more important than marriage. It is a relationship with Christ, the Bridegroom. He is the One who is there no matter what, who listens to your heart's cry even in the middle of the night. He is the One who makes no emotional demands. He just loves you because He loves you. Earthly marriage is not the answer for your heart's needs.

MARRIAGE-MYTH SPIN-OFFS

Marriage is a wonderful institution established by God for a purpose. It was His intent from the beginning that marriage would be the place where man and woman would come together in a supportive relationship, where children would be conceived and nurtured, where the world would see a picture of Christ and His bride, the church. However, Jesus Christ did not come to die for marriages. He came to die for people. There is a big difference between the institution that was created to do good for man and to represent God and the people who are in that institution. Like the law that was made for man, marriage is made for people. It is to be honored, respected, held to, and defended, but when people become hapless victims of outra geous behavior within that marriage, it is time to say, "Hold it! What are we defending here?"

This is one of the saddest myths I have seen floating around. With the words "God hates divorce" many significant marital issues are shelved. Those who are suffering are often told by their church leadership to go home and pray. In other words, because God hates divorce, we are not going to face any problems that might lead to the creation of a crisis! There seems to be a fear that a crisis might lead to the breaking of the marriage, and then we might face a divorce. There seems to be more fear of divorce than of what is happening to people behind closed doors.

A precious woman I met at a conference was the walking picture of just such a situation. She was poor but noble. She had five children and a husband who refused to work. She did what she could to feed her family and keep them clothed and schooled, but every day was a struggle. I asked her if she had gone to the church to help solve this marital conflict that looked so hopeless. "Yes," she said quietly. "They just sent me home and told me to pray."

"Did they speak to your husband?" I asked.

"No," was her sad and very hopeless answer.

That is what myths do. They leave you hopeless.

God hates divorce, but He equally hates the obscenity of arrogant behavior that causes damage to another human being. Look with me at what is written in Malachi 2:13–16. I am giving it to you in *The Amplified Version* because it seems to shed more light on what is being said:

> And this you do with double guilt; you cover the altar of the Lord with your tears [shed by your unoffending wives, divorced by you that you might take heathen wives], and with your own weeping and crying out because the Lord does not regard your offering any more or accept it with favor at your hand. Yet you ask, Why does He reject it? Because the Lord was witness [to the covenant made at your marriage] between you and the wife of your youth, against whom you have dealt treacherously and to whom you were faithless. Yet she is your companion and the wife of your covenant [made by your marriage vows]. And did God not make [you and your wife] one [flesh]? Did not One make you and preserve your spirit alive? And why did God make you two one? Because He sought a godly offspring [from your union]. Therefore take heed to yourselves, and let no one deal treacherously and be faithless to the wife of his youth. For the Lord, the God of Israel says: I hate divorce and

marital separation, and him who covers his garment [his wife], with violence. Therefore keep a watch upon your spirit [that it may be controlled by My Spirit], that you deal not treacherously and faithlessly [with your marriage mate].

God always goes to the heart of the matter, which is people and their relationship to Him and to one another. The institution of marriage is not the heart of the matter, but people are. So, if we are going to look at marriage with His heart of compassion as well as His piercing eye of truth, we have to stop hanging on to myths that toss us in all directions. We can't just say, "Well, God hates divorce," and thus deify marriage over the two people in the union who may be suffering. Nor can we say, "Well, it never works, so why bother?" That belittles a God-ordained institution.

God had a great and noble purpose in marriage. You can see why He started out with a simple plan: leave, cleave, become one flesh. His goal was to have a godly offspring. (By the way, that is why the sexual union is so important and creates such trauma when it is handled carelessly. Do you use sex for leverage? Does your mate? If so, you are tampering with something God takes very seriously.) When we add to or take away from God's plan, we buy right into the Enemy's scheme and embrace that now-familiar myth, *God is holding out on me and doesn't mean what He says.*

"ARISE MY DARLING, MY BEAUTIFUL ONE, AND COME ALONG!"

Marriage does not make everything wonderful. It has high responsibility and extensive commitment. You can live married and be fulfilled, and you can live single and be fulfilled. The choice of how you live is up to you. Your marriage partner or the lack thereof has no control over your spirit and your relationship to the Lord. It is true that your marriage partner can bring you joy or sorrow in your day-to-day life, but how you respond is all within your power.

How many times have I sat and listened to a wife complain that her husband doesn't understand her, doesn't meet her needs, and is totally absent emotionally. Everything she says may be absolutely true, but all her sadness, anger, and complaining is not going to change those characteristics in her husband. For whatever reason, he has made a choice to behave the way he does. Instead of lamenting what she doesn't have and probably will never have, the wife has just as much choice as her mate.

A wife must realize her life does not rest on her husband's adoration, acceptance, or understanding. Her future is not tied to his ability or ingenuity. Her emotional, spiritual, and physical well-being are her responsibility alone. If he fulfills the role of a "virtuous husband," then she is blessed. If he does not, then she is still blessed. She may be challenged, but in that challenge there is still a blessing. It is all in her perspective. In fact, that is true with everything that happens to us.

It is that well-worn axiom: It is not what happens to us that matters, but what we think about what happens to us.

That idea may confuse you if you fail to remember that the truth that God is not holding out on us, and He *does* mean what He says. If that is true, then a marriage that is lackluster does not mean a life that is lackluster. It all depends on what you decide to do with it.

Now let me be perfectly clear. Lacking luster does not mean abusive. It does not mean that you are demeaned, harshly treated, or physically pushed around, slapped, or beaten. That is a different scenario, and it requires swift action to stop it. That is why we have laws, and since "the law is for the lawless" (1 Timothy 1:9), use whatever resources you have at your command to bring such behavior to an immediate halt. The longer it goes on, the worse it gets. If you have that kind of marriage, God is not holding out on you, and He does mean what He says—and He has installed laws and rulers to take care of that kind of nonsense. It is for your protection, so don't hesitate to rely on them.

If you are in a situation where you have nothing in common, except maybe the children, and you are hurt and disappointed because you have not gotten what you wanted and you don't feel fulfilled, then you have options. The greatest option of all is recognizing that life is not about marriage or about being loved and wonderfully supported by a mate who cares deeply. As wonderful as that is, remember that it can vanish at any given moment for any number of reasons. What you *can* count on is the deep, deep love of Jesus.

Now, don't check out on me here. I know we all are like the little child who wanted Jesus to have "skin on." What we touch and see is far more convincing to us than what we sense, believe, and understand. But think about it. What is the one constant, abiding, unchanging factor in your life? Jesus. Who is the one who can control what you think and feel? You. There you have the combination that is the most significant. As you relate to Him as the perfect friend, companion, and lover, the disappointment of earthly love takes on a whole new view.

You are probably saying to yourself, "Nice words, but how do I do that?"

This is how! Yes, it can be done, and it is wonderful to experience.

You begin to pursue a relationship with Jesus just as you would with a warm, responsive, caring mate. You start by telling Him everything—good, bad, and indifferent. You reveal the secret or even not-so-secret issues of your heart. If it matters to you, tell Him about it. If the refrigerator breaks, tell Jesus how inconvenient that is. If your children are sick, ask Jesus to comfort and heal them. If your boss is a bear, tell Jesus how you hate it when he acts that way and how you would like to just walk out. If your husband has been cold and distant, tell Jesus. Tell Him everything. You don't have to sugarcoat it, put it in Standard English, or even (heaven forbid) in Old English with a bunch of Thees and Thous. All you have to do is to begin to talk to Him. Amazingly, when you are quiet, you will begin to hear Him responding to you. The more you pour out your heart, the more you will long to pick up His book and read what He says to you. It is set in stone. It will never change. It is never based on His mood. It is truth that will hold you when everything around you is couched in smoke and mirrors.

When you are the most lonely or are hurt by a mate who is just "not there," you can retreat to the beautiful words of the Song of Solomon. If you want to know how Jesus feels about you, this is it!

> "I am the rose of Sharon,
> The lily of the valleys."

> "Like a lily among the thorns,
> So is my darling among the maidens."

"Like an apple tree among the trees of the forest,
So is my beloved among the young men.
In his shade I took great delight and sat down,
And his fruit was sweet to my taste.
He has brought me to his banquet hall,
And his banner over me is love."
— SONG OF SOLOMON 2:1–4

"My beloved responded and said to me,
'Arise, my darling, my beautiful one,
And come along.
For behold, the winter is past,
The rain is over and gone.
The flowers have already appeared in the land;
The time has arrived for pruning the vines,
And the voice of the turtledove has been heard in our land.
The fig tree has ripened its figs,
And the vines in blossom have given forth their fragrance.
Arise, my darling, my beautiful one,
And come along!'"
— SONG OF SOLOMON 2:10–13

No matter what your marriage is like or not like, you can have more love, understanding, and passion in your life than you could ever dream. The Lover of your soul, the One who will never change is calling you. "Arise, my darling, my beautiful one, and come along!"

CHAPTER SIX

THE MYTH OF HAPPY LITTLE WOMEN

"Can she bake a cherry pie, Billy Boy, Billy Boy?
"Can she bake a cherry pie, Charming Billy?
"She can bake a cherry pie quick as a cat can wink its eye,
"She's a young thing and cannot leave her Mother." (NURSERY RHYME)

B illy Boy had a problem. He had a potential wife who was a "young thing" and couldn't leave her mamma! Truth is, the woman had a problem too. She could do some grown-up things, such as baking pies, but she couldn't leave home. She had not yet grown up in all ways.

If you are to be a fully functioning woman, you have to be an adult woman. That's the way God intended it. Before He formed you in your mother's womb, He had a plan for you (Psalm 139), and unless He numbered your days to end in childhood, He intended for you to grow up and become a woman. Maturity is His goal for all His human creations, especially for His children, His Christians (1 Corinthians 14:20).

We have a problem in a system that has perverted the original pattern and thwarted full maturity for women. Even women who are mature are often expected to behave like children if they want to be "appropriate." A hierarchical system that puts women in a role of silence and mindless compliance was never God's intent—"Where is it written?"—but the culture has created and allowed such mythical arrangements to flourish.

There are only a few rules in the Scriptures about order and a woman's place in that order, but some people have magnified those Scriptures and made them a code for "keeping women in their place." And cultural attitudes create an environment where often putting women down occurs without premeditation—it just happens.

In *A Confident, Dynamic You,* Marie Chapian gives two poignant illustrations that make the point.

A very talented and accomplished musician friend of mine was told as a child that if she didn't stop playing the piano she'd never get a boyfriend. This same woman, who now thrills millions with her music, recently told me that after one of her concerts in our city, a young lady said to her, "I'll bet men are really intimidated by a female as brilliant and talented as you are, right?"

How are we supposed to feel good about ourselves if who we are is somehow intimidating? . . . The message my friend received was that she was not being what she was supposed to be, unintimidating, or I suppose "unbrilliant" is more like it.

Just recently I received a call from a man giving me advice on buying real estate. "Now remember, Marie, try not to think like a woman!" he said. I asked him what, in his opinion, did a woman think like?

"Oh, you know. Women don't think with their heads, they think with their emotions. They aren't tough enough. Women need to think more like men."[1]

Whatever that is.

The truth is we have to live life out of our personalities, giftedness, and gender. God has made us who we are and the way we are, so to suppress these areas of our lives in order to fit into a system is a denial of who God made us to be.

Some of us "think like men" and often are put down because of it. Some of us think like men and have a leadership gift as well. When those gifts are exercised in the working world, we are well paid for them. Unfortunately, in some Christian circles, when we exercise the very same gifts with the same attitude and level of competency, we are viewed as a threat.

Of course, I think this is a good time to ask, "Where is it written?"

Now I am not questioning the order that God has established for the family and for the church. He has established that order, and what He does is right. His order works because it has mutual responsibility built in. I am speaking instead of the mythical mind-set that keeps women trying to figure out how to be who God made them to be and yet fit into the cultural mores of the church. It is hard to be the woman described in Proverbs 31:16–17 and at the same time a woman viewed as nonthreatening and therefore safe.

> *She considers a field and buys it;*
> *From her earnings she plants a vineyard.*
> *She girds herself with strength*
> *And makes her arms strong.*
> *She senses that her gain is good;*
> *Her lamp does not go out at night.*

Because of the many conflicting messages we receive and because we have found that it works, sometimes women resort to being "little women." This is a little girl walking around in an adult body. This is the woman who is convinced that the best way to get along is to stay small in mind and helpless in attitude. She has discovered that there are men who like that demeanor and will give her what she wants when she exhibits it.

Men aren't the only ones who like her that way. Many powerful people like for their employees to be unquestioning little girls, and sometimes even aging parents like for daughters to be little, no matter how old they are. To see that stated on paper seems stark, but think about it, and see if you think it is true, if not in your own life at least in the lives of some women close to you.

WHAT DO LITTLE WOMEN LOOK LIKE?

Here is a profile of a little woman. See what you think.

A little woman is insecure.

She has learned that a helpless demeanor is more effective than a confident one. She has been told all her life that men don't like overpowering women. That is true, but it is not only men who don't like overpowering women. No one likes them. But no one likes overpowering men, either. The point is that there is a myth about strong, decisive, "know who they are" women that hangs at the edges of our cultural thought. If you know who you are and act like it, often you are labeled as a feminist—and that throws cold water in the face of many sincere Christian women. They feel they have to suppress their personalities and limit the use of their gifts. They would prefer to act like little women and be considered good Christian role models than to fight the criticism and prejudice that will result if they act like adult persons.

Interestingly, some of us have reverted to being little women and haven't even recognized what has happened to us. It is never too late to change, so if you see yourself in any of these descriptions, mark it and determine before God that you are going to grow into the adult woman He intended.

A little woman needs lots of reassurance.

A little woman really likes it if someone else will assume responsibility. She has come to understand that to take responsibility will mean she could be criticized—and the last thing a little woman can stand is to be questioned or criticized. She needs people around her to go with her everywhere. It doesn't feel right to her to go to a movie alone, shop alone, or make a decision without asking for the opinion of several others. She doesn't trust her own thought processes, so she looks for other people to affirm her.

A little woman relates to her husband like a father.

"I have to ask my husband." This is not the spirit of fitting in that is part of a godly woman's responsibility. This is the fearful, "afraid to make Daddy mad" mind-set of a little girl. This is not asking your mate about his plans so that your plans will not conflict and can be compatible. It is asking permission like a child and anxiously waiting for him to say yes or no.

A little woman believes that her husband should handle all the money.

She either believes money is too adult and complicated for her, or she believes that she can spend money without having to worry about it. Daddy-husband will take care of the bills. The third spin on the money issue is that she would like to earn enough to "buy a field," but knows that if she did, it would be threatening to her husband. So she goes along, making minor purchases for the household but leaving the big buys—and very often the big ideas—to Daddy-husband. It is very hard for a little woman to have her own checkbook, especially if Daddy-husband doesn't think she should have her own money.

A little woman might like to grow past her girlish relationship with her husband, but change scares her and threatens him.

She fears that if she grows up Daddy–husband won't take care of her anymore. He will be upset if she changes, so it is easier to stay a little woman. The losses seem too great to her if she changes.

A little woman makes a good mother when she can play or show off her children in parades or beauty pageants.

She fades into helplessness when her children really need her. She becomes one of the children and hopes that Daddy-husband, or some other adult in the family, will step up to the plate and help her out. The children are too much, and they run rampant. She can corral them at times with a little yelling and smacking, but they can easily get her flustered. Those are the days she wants to run rampant too. Sometimes she even threatens to run away because of the children. Daddy-husband and life are just too hard. Sometimes she does leave, but not so far that Daddy-husband locks the door. She doesn't want to lose him in the process—she needs him.

A little woman relates to God like she does to Daddy-husband.

When God does what she likes, she is demonstrative in her thank-yous. She is emotional and ebullient in her praise for all to see. When God says, "Wait," or "Later," or, heaven forbid, "No," she turns into a two-year-old on a rampage. She pouts, cries, and looks for any indulgent adult she can find to pity her plight. She doesn't mind letting everyone know that she is mad at God. She is inconsolable and refuses to look at God's character or sovereign will. She repeats her disappointment to all and is annoyed if anyone points out that she might be in the wrong.

A little woman has trouble going deep with God because that requires work.

A little woman doesn't think she can study—she doesn't think she can find the time. A little woman thinks people who do that are great, but she doesn't see herself in those ranks. A little woman has trouble making a commitment to anything. She has things to do and something always comes up, so she can't say that she will do anything for sure.

A little woman never questions what is taught in church.

Well, actually, she rarely listens very deeply. About the only thing she really gets anything out of is the music—she does enjoy that. She is easily bored, and her mind wanders when it comes to the Word. Occasionally, though, she hears something that makes her feel so guilty that she cries and nods her head and promises to do better. A little woman would like to know more, but she sees herself as limited in her ability to understand.

A little woman doesn't believe that God really made her for any-thing special anyway, so if she doesn't fulfill some huge destiny, that's OK with her.

She is happy with things that satisfy for a while until she can get some more things. The decor in her home is rarely ever settled unless Daddy-husband puts down his foot. Then she pouts and is unhappy. Daddy-husband is annoying to her, and yet she maintains a dependency that keeps them tightly knit together in their mutual pain. Neither little woman nor Daddy-husband thinks she or he can or need to change, so seeking counseling or pursuing growth is just not in their realm of thought.

This particular element of the little woman myth goes right to the core of who you are, so it will cause as much pain as all the others combined. If you see yourself as an underdeveloped female who has reached maturity physically but is still small in the mind and heart, then you are in a deep pond scum and it is time to try to wade out. It is your choice, and you have the power if you are a Christian. You can do it. It may feel really strange at first, but you have what it takes to begin to live as the adult woman God has created you to be. It is exciting to think of the possibilities.

A little woman has allowed the "little woman" myth to get all tangled up with the "God wants me to be a big girl" myth.

When it comes draining the joy of life, all that conniving devil, Satan, has to do is cross the wires of our understanding. The very quality God desires of us in relation to *Him,* many of us have adopted in our relationship to *people.* God wants us to be like little children when we come to Him, but adults as we relate to the world, the church, and our mates. We have turned it around and have chosen to relate as confident, well-informed adults when we speak to God (telling Him what needs to happen) and little women (needy of someone to help) when we relate to the world. No wonder we are in a mess!

Let's look at the Scriptures and see what God says about "little woman" and "big girl." Jesus was making a point in Matthew 18:2–6, when this scene occurred:

And He called a child to Himself and set him before them, and said, "Truly I say to you, unless you are converted and become like children, you will not enter the kingdom of heaven. Whoever then humbles himself as this child, he is the greatest in the kingdom of heaven. And whoever receives one such child in My name receives Me; but whoever causes one of these little ones who believe in Me to stumble, it would be better for him to have a heavy millstone hung around his neck, and to be drowned in the depth of the sea."

And, in Matthew 19:13–15, we see another scene with children:

Then some children were brought to Him so that He might lay His hands on them and pray; and the disciples rebuked them. But Jesus said, "Let the children alone, and do not hinder them from coming to Me; for the kingdom of heaven belongs to such as these." After laying His hands on them, He departed from there.

We are to come to Christ as little children. There is no room for big girl to show up and take over. We come to our Father to be one of His children. We don't come to him in fear and trembling, but we do come as ones who have been adopted into His family. We are His; we are longed for; and we are desired.

———————————— ✠ ————————————

DANIEL WEBSTER AND A CHILD'S PRAYER

G. H. Morling writes: "I find that men who have been long in the School of Jesus become simpler and simpler in their attitude towards the Heavenly Father. I find that they become as little children. Late in his life, Daniel Webster, as he prepared for sleep, used to offer the child's prayer beginning: Now I lay me down to sleep, I pray the Lord my soul to keep."

G. H. Morling, The Quest for Serenity *(Nashville: Word, 1989), 51.*

———————————— ✠ ————————————

In biblical times there was an Aramaic term of endearment that was only used for close family. It was similar to our word for daddy. In the Scriptures we read it as "Abba." Look at what Paul wrote in Romans 8:15–17:

> *For you have not received a spirit of slavery leading to fear again, but you have received a spirit of adoption as sons by which we cry out, "Abba! Father!" The Spirit Himself testifies with our spirit that we are children of God, and if children, heirs also, heirs of God and fellow heirs with Christ.*

As we relate to our heavenly Father it is appropriate, desired, and needful for us to become like a child—a child who needs to be cared for, nurtured, protected, and encouraged. That is our relationship to God. If we think we are going to relate to Him any other way, we will be sorely disappointed. We just can't come to Him as an adult equal, thinking that somehow we are going to convincingly reason with Him. He does not desire that in us. He did not desire that in His Son. He wants to relate to us as a beloved Daddy. He is *Abba,* our beloved, holy Daddy!

When Jesus walked this earth, think about the way He related to the Father. He was the Son. When He was in the most difficult hour of His life, in the Garden of Gethsemane in total agony, look at what He called out.

> *And He was saying, "Abba! Father! All things are possible for You; remove this cup from Me; yet not what I will, but what You will."* (MARK 14:36)

"Daddy, please. You can do it for me . . . but not what I want, what you want!" That was their relationship, and it is a picture of how our Abba Father wants to relate to us. If you have entered into a relationship with the Father by admitting that you cannot save yourself, that you have sinned, that you need a Savior, and that you have accepted the fact that Jesus is the Way, the Truth, and the Life, then you can and should relate to God as a child—a little girl who needs the provision and care of her Daddy.

You don't have to be an adult in His presence. Adulthood is what you wear when you walk through your daily life. Interestingly enough, it is only as you become a little woman in response to God that you can become an adult woman—or a big girl—in relationship to the world. If you have spent time with your heavenly Father and have gained understanding from Him, you can face any relationship you have with the grace of an adult woman.

How like Satan, the deceiver, to try to confuse us on that issue! Remember, when he messes with our minds, he just wants to make us believe that God is holding out on us and that He doesn't mean what He says. It is characteristic of the deceiver to suggest that we should be little-girl-like in our relationships on earth, but strong, bold, and big-girl-like when we talk to our Father. What a sly, sneaky snake. He thought he could be pretty "large and in charge" in the presence of God, and he would like for us to make the same awful mistake. He is crawling on his belly, eating dust. It would suit him just fine for us to do the same thing in our relationships.

GROWN UP, BIG GIRL—ADULT!

God the Father created us and He packed each of us with potential that would be unleashed as we grew up. As we take in the milk of the Word—the first principles—then move to solid meat and go through life's circumstances, we become more and more the adult women God intended us to be. His desire for us is that we would pursue growing into mature women of God, women who are strong, who know truth, and who manage their lives well. See what He says in Hebrews that is directed toward people who won't get away from the milk of the Word, who find it a challenge to do the hard things, who just want to hold on to the milk.

> *For everyone who partakes only of milk is not accustomed to the word of righteousness, for he is an infant. But solid food is for the mature, who because of practice have their senses trained to discern good and evil.* (HEBREWS 5:13–14)

The milk drinkers are the little women who go to church week after week, hear the same message (or at least perceive that they are hearing the same message), sing a few praise songs, and then go home and live the same way they have always lived. They are unhappy and confused. If you could peer into their minds, you would see these words emblazoned: "God is holding out on me, and God doesn't mean what He says." If you peered into their relationships, you would see elements of little woman popping up from time to time. Their lives don't look much different from those of the women they spend time with at work or with whom they sit on the sidelines of a soccer game. They are all little women who are not truly happy but are afraid to challenge the way things are for fear that they might lose.

Sometimes little women cannot even tell good from evil. As a result they end up in messes they never intended to get into. God warns about what happens to little women in 2 Timothy 3:6–7. He says that there will be people who will "enter into households and captivate weak women weighed down with sins, led on by various impulses, always learning and never able to come to the knowledge of the truth." Interestingly the Greek word for "women" in this passage is in the diminutive form. It means that there are little women who are targets for deception because they are laden down with sins. They run on their impulses. They make a stab at learning, but if it requires too much, they won't pursue it.

Libby attended church and wanted a Christian influence for her two girls. She and Kevin had a rocky relationship, but at least they went to church together and loved their kids with an equal passion. Libby's job kept her in contact with Jack, a guy she could talk to better than Kevin. Libby and Jack became friends, then best friends.

One night when they were working late on an inventory project, the unthinkable happened—Libby and Jack became lovers. Libby was horrified because she never meant for that to happen. She needed a friend, she thought, but she didn't want a lover.

The next day she couldn't look Kevin in the eye. She was teary, and when he asked her what was wrong, she sobbed and told him everything. Both of them had taken in only a little "milk" of the Word, so they were not mature enough to handle this huge assault on their marriage. (Remember the one-flesh issue? Their one-flesh union had been broken. Oh, they were still one flesh, but now there was another person in the picture who complicated things terribly. Jack! What to do about Jack?)

Kevin crumbled. His and Libby's marriage wasn't strong enough to stand the breaking of the "one flesh" commitment. Libby went into a depression of self-loathing for which there was no consolation. And Jack . . . well, bless his heart . . . Jack began to talk because Libby pulled away from him. He felt scorned, so he paid Libby back by giving tidbits of information to a few of their friends at work.

Libby was unable to recognize good and evil at a time when someone whose senses had been exercised by the Word would have picked up on the problem. Jack was too available, too willing to listen, too sympathetic. Libby saw him as a friend. A big girl would have spotted that there was potential in the friendship for more than met the eye. Big girls know when to avoid situations that can be compromising.

I will always thank my parents for protecting me in a situation that could have been less than wholesome. My brand-new husband was in Vietnam. We had a baby, and I worked nights at a department store while my parents kept the baby. One night I came home and announced innocently that four of us were going to go to dinner the next week. My parents asked me who the other three were. When they found out there were two young men and another young woman, they suggested that I think about what I was planning to do. I was going to dinner in what looked like a double-date situation. I didn't see it that way and protested loudly that that was not what it was. We were just four friends going to dinner.

Now one of the men was married, but his wife wasn't going. My husband was in Vietnam, so he wasn't going. The other woman was single, so it was not a problem for her. My parents wisely pointed out that although my intentions may have been innocent—and they were—the appearance was not good. I was not a Christian at that point, so my senses had not been exercised to recognize some of the more subtle forms of evil. But I did know that when my parents pointed out something to me, I needed to at least think about it. I did think about it, and the next night told my dinner pals that I wouldn't be able to go.

Now that I am more mature and my senses have been exercised to know good from evil, I am grateful that my parents sent up a red flag. Granted, nothing probably would have happened that would have been compromising, but since I didn't go, there was definitely no harm done.

Big girls, or real women, or whatever you want to call them, learn to make choices with the big picture in mind. Little women look at the moment and react to whatever they see. The Word of God, as well as life, teaches adult women what they need to know to be successful. Little women rarely learn because they don't see the problem. When you have been on "milk" too long that's what happens!

> *Brethren [and Sisteren] do not be children in your thinking; yet in evil be infants, but in your thinking be mature.* (1 CORINTHIANS 14:20)

That is a pretty strong word. Now I realize that not everyone will hear it, heed it, or care one whit about it, but if you want to be a fully developed adult woman who lives life well, this is your choice.

THE MAP OUT OF LITTLE WOMANVILLE

The reality is that you have to live life, and as you live, you grow if you are an adult. Little women don't grow because that means change, and change is fearful to little women unless they are creating the change in their own safe shell. Changes like hair color, makeup, clothing, and decor are OK for little women as long as those changes fit in with what everyone else is doing. Little women resist change. That is why they stay little women.

Then there are adult women who have maintained an immature demeanor because they haven't seen that there is a way to be the adults they are without running amuck of existing mores in society and in the church. That is a stuck place to be. Nowhere in Scripture can I find a place where women are to be less than adult. The Scriptures that encourage all believers to be mature, stable, and single-minded include women. So there is no way to stay a little woman if you want to be God's woman. But how do you change?

There is a wonderful verse in the context of spiritual gifts and love that is like a map out of Little Womanville! It is 1 Corinthians 13:11:

> *"When I was a child, I used to speak like a child, think like a child, reason like a child; when I became a man [or a woman], I did away with childish things."*

If you have seen yourself as a little woman and want to change, even if that means giving up some things, you can. You don't have to continue to live in a way you don't want to live. Remember, you can't change the people around you, but you can change how you respond to them.

Put Away Childish Speaking

You can do away with childish things. For instance, you can do away with speaking childishly. If you have something to say, use words that communicate what you really think. Put away sarcasm, innuendo, whining, and pouting. Say what you think is important—say it clearly, kindly, succinctly, and take all the childish emotion out of it. You may think that you won't be able to get your point across. Oh, yes, you will! Say what you want to say like an adult, and you will be heard.

One of the reasons we fear we won't be heard is that we have trained people to listen a certain way. We have fallen into the rut of believing that they only will hear our message in only one form. In reality, if we speak in a clear, adult way, they will be *more* prone to hear what we are saying. They may not like it anymore, but if in the past you trained people to listen to a whine, when you begin to speak with straightforward words they will be surprised—and perk up and hear you.

Put Away Sparring

One of the ways you can hear yourself and, therefore, begin to correct the way you talk is to leave a tape recorder going in your kitchen when there are people around. You will soon forget its presence, talk naturally, and hear yourself as you sound to others. Then you can begin to change what you say and how you say it.

I have been on the radio for a number of years, and I can tell you that I don't enjoy listening to myself after I finish. I usually want to move on rather than look back at what I have recorded, but it has been very helpful for me to listen to myself from time to time. I hear the things I say and the way I say them, and I am amazed. I don't mean to sound abrupt, argumentative, or abrasive, and yet if I hear that

I sound that way, it pains me—and I can change. You can do the same. That is the wonderful part about becoming an adult woman. You can change. It is your prerogative, and it is in your power! That, to me, is one of the best parts of being an adult! I can leave behind the immature things I don't want to carry around any longer!

Let me tell you something you can put away that you may not even recognize in your speech. The only reason I recognize it is because I know that I do it. It is called "sparring," a childish form of point-counterpoint. Sadly for me, I am very good at this and I find that I can confuse an issue pretty quickly with rapid-fire counterpoint responses. After I have fallen into one of these exchanges, I always ask myself why I thought it was necessary. I find that it is always because I haven't been able to get my point across, so out of frustration I begin to spar. Well, that gets me nowhere but angry.

Put Away Childish Methods

You never make a point adult to adult by using childish methods. You can know that you have slipped into using childish methods by the way you feel afterwards. Do you feel thwarted? Angry? Maybe you feel a little like pouting? Then you have employed a method of communication that has not worked. The point is to speak the truth—and to speak it well and convincingly. Then you have to leave the hearing and the response to the other person. You don't have to go on and on like a child. Say what you have to say, say it with the grace of a woman, and then, with the self-respect of an adult, expect a response. It may not be what you want, but if you speak as an adult and act as if you expect a response, more often than not, you will get one. It is all about recognizing where we trap ourselves in little woman ways and how we can begin to change!

Little women say what they want to say any way they want to say it. Or, sometimes little women don't say anything for fear of being rejected. Adult women keep the goal in mind: to get the point communicated! That means considering the ears of the hearer and what is needed in order to be heard. It also includes making sure that the call for a response is clearly understood.

Exception

There is a time when an adult woman is not in a position to speak and convince. All of her convincing has to be done through a *quiet spirit*. It takes an adult woman to believe that God knows what is best when dealing with a man who does not obey the Word.

> *In the same way, you wives, be submissive to your own husbands so that even if any of them are disobedient to the word, they may be won without a word by the behavior of their wives, as they observe your chaste and respectful behavior. Your adornment must not be merely external—braiding the hair, and wearing gold jewelry, or putting on dresses; but let it be the hidden person of the heart, with the imperishable quality of a gentle and quiet spirit, which is precious in the sight of God.* (1 PETER 3:1–4)

A little woman struggles with a God who works behind the scenes. She wants to make sure that everything is "happening"—and happening *now*—because she is uncomfortable with this "gag order." Her husband needs to know that he is being disobedient. If she doesn't tell him, who will?

You know you are growing up when you can let God take care of His job, and you take care of yours. A little woman really struggles with this. But these struggles can lead somewhere. As she gets more and more uncomfortable and becomes convinced that it is no longer worthwhile to think and reason as a child, a little woman may learn what it means to become an adult woman.

Remember, it is circumstances and the Word that mingle to give us a new paradigm. We were born babies and raised little girls, and the transition to adult women is a leap over a great abyss for some. Some make the leap, take a deep breath, and live as growing adults for all the rest of their days. Some slip into the abyss and spend much of their lives crawling up the sides, straightening their crinolines, rubbing soot off their cheeks, and whining about the pains of being an adult! That is a little woman.

I don't know about you, but given the option I always will choose the big girl, adult woman option. The immediate challenge may be greater than what a little woman has to face, but the payoff in the end is a life well-lived and lives impacted for eternity. A little woman will have an impact, but it will be a temporary irritation to those she loves. Her weaknesses and self-centered behavior will inevitably cause pain for herself and others.

The myth of little woman is just that—a myth. It is a myth to think that you can live as less than God intended and be fulfilled. It is a myth to think that a little woman cannot change. The question is, *will* she? If you have seen yourself as a little woman, are you willing to begin the process? Are you willing to start peeling off the pinafores and putting on the clothes of a woman?

You can do it! You just have to look in the proverbial mirror and recognize that the old clothes don't fit. When you left elementary school and headed for middle school, I bet there was no way you would have been caught dead in the childish clothes of grade school days. You wanted to dress the part for what you were becoming

I want to encourage you to not become discouraged if you are well into your years and yet you still see yourself living as a little woman. It is never too late to change, and there is nothing more wonderful than a woman who is willing to face her need and willing to try. You will stumble and fall on your knees from time to time. That's OK. Get up and keep going.

It is like learning to roller skate (I guess it would be cooler to talk about roller blades, but I bet you probably relate to the "skate" picture!). You start to skate, you fall, you get up . . . you start to skate, you fall, you get up. But one day, you find that you can skate. The better you get at it, the more confident you become and the better you feel about yourself. The more accomplished you become, the more respect you get from the other skaters. They stay out of your way because they don't want to make you stumble—and get this—they want to skate just like you!

Wow! Think what it would be like to have other little women looking at you saying, "I want to be an adult woman just like her!" It can happen. So wherever you are, don't be discouraged. Just tell the Lord you want to be a child in His eyes and that you need Him desperately. Ask Him to give you the courage to become an adult woman, and then determine that is who you will be by His grace! It will take time, but you can do it. While you are in the process, cling to these words of comfort from the dear apostle Paul: "Forgetting those things that are behind, I press on!"

The following poem has been a favorite of mine for years. I found it at a time I was making a giant leap over a wide abyss. I was confronted with a decision that would impact everything in my world. The decision was hard, but when I made it and took the running leap, I found this poem, and it touched something very tender and vulnerable in my growing-up heart. If you want to become an adult woman, it will speak to you, I have no doubt. And if you are already there, it will comfort you in the choices you have made and in the good-byes you have spoken.

- COMES THE DAWN -

After a while you learn the subtle difference
Between holding a hand and chaining a soul,
And you learn that love doesn't mean leaning
And company doesn't mean security,
And you begin to understand that kisses aren't contracts
And presents aren't promises,
And you begin to accept your defeats
With your head held high and your eyes open,
With the grace of a woman, not the grief of a child.

You learn to build your roads
On today because tomorrow's ground
Is too uncertain for plans, and futures have
A way of falling down in mid-flight.
After a while you learn that even sunshine
Burns if you get too much,
So you plant your own garden and decorate
Your own soul, instead of waiting
For someone to bring you flowers.

And you learn that you really can endure,

That you really are strong
And you really have worth
And you learn and learn . . . and you learn
With every good-bye, you learn.

—AUTHOR UNKNOWN

CHAPTER SEVEN

THE MYTH OF DIVORCE IS THE END

G od hates divorce!" It breaks His heart. That is truth. That is not a myth.

Divorce is a sad, gut-wrenching result of all that happened in the Garden of Eden. Adam and Eve were turned in different directions when they chose to turn away from God and do their own thing. From that day on, relationship would be a struggle. Oneness was shattered.

After the Fall, marriage would be there to give the first couple restored oneness as they committed to leave, cleave, and become one flesh. That was the picture of a relationship intended to last forever. That was, and is, God's heart. That was, and is, God's plan. And, for most people who get married, that is their plan as well. It is a rare person who marries believing that it will shortly be over. The statistics are grim, but nevertheless, most marry thinking, "We are the exception. Our love will endure."

The pain comes when the reality of irreconcilable issues crops up. Even among those who claim to be Christians, things happen that shatter dreams and dash hopes. I am not talking about the adjustments that are part and parcel of the marriage contract: trying to share the bathroom, putting the cap on the toothpaste tube, or underdone chicken. I'm talking about issues of the heart that pierce to the very soul of a relationship. I am talking about the situations that cry out for the answer to the question "What do I do?"

- John claimed to be a Christian, but shortly after their marriage, his wife stumbled upon files and files of pornographic material in their computer. Devastated, she confronted him and asked what was going on. He became defensive and sullen. From that day on, he was a different man. He refused to talk about the pornography. He became a stranger to Susan. He no longer laughed with her or even talked with her. She had become the enemy. All counseling was spurned. She prayed and prayed, but John became ever more encased in his cold, uncaring response to her. Susan was faced with what many others ask: "What do I do?"

- Arnie slept with Cecile three times after their marriage. After the first week, he told her she wasn't what he wanted and he carefully avoided touching her. At first, Cecile cried and then she began to go for help. No matter what she did or what she tried, it didn't matter. Arnie was sexually finished with her. He was pleasant enough. He went to work and sat next to her in church, but that was about it between them. He refused to talk to anyone about it. This was the way it was, and that was that. Cecile's question four years later was the same as that of the others: "What do I do?"

- Karen adored Mike, but when he drank, she was terrified. He became belligerent and broke up furniture. The first few times he did it, she told no one and waited for the storm to blow over. Then they had a child. Hearing her baby scream because Daddy was throwing dishes was too much. She left and went to her mother's. Mike cried and asked her to come back when he sobered up. She returned, but it happened again and again. One night he went too far and hit her. As far as she knew he was sexually faithful, but life with Mike was beyond endurance. She moved out and stayed out this time. Her question: "What to do?"
  Each of these situations is complex and filled with elements that

are too many to include. Each is true, with the names and details changed to protect the people involved. I could repeat story after story of broken, insane situations. Since this is a book for women, I have spoken only of women who have been wounded. The reality is that these situations run both ways.

My point is that trouble is all around us. Pain is harsh and unrelenting in many marriages. Some marriages are the way they are because a woman deliberately went against what she knew to be true and married an unbeliever, hoping that somehow she could influence him to become a Christian. Some are that way because a mate masqueraded as a Christian in order to get what he wanted. Some are that way because neither one knew what he was doing. Now that it is done, they are in a big mess they don't know how to fix. If you are caught in such a situation, you are wondering, "What do I do?"

DIVORCE IS NOT THE END

The most important step to take when you encounter something you absolutely don't have a clue about is to go with what you do know. Unfortunately, many of us are walking around draped in mythical thinking because we don't really know what we think we know. We know what we have been told—and if you have ever encountered trouble in your marriage and looked for help, in most church settings you have been told, "God hates divorce." Everything else is predicated on that one statement. Often, although you may get some sound advice, the "God hates divorce" statement is so huge you can't get beyond it. God does hate divorce, and I don't know many people who like divorce either, especially those who are going through it! It is hard, gut-wrenching, and always leaves scars. There is no way you can enter into a covenant relationship, become one flesh with another individual, even have children with that person, and think you can walk away unscarred. God hates divorce because the scars on His children are deep and ugly. But He is a God of compassion, and He allows divorce when the scars within the confines of marriage are deeper and uglier than divorce. Divorce is an ugly reality of our fallen state. If we were all still in Eden, there would be no divorce, but our hearts have hardened toward God and one another and, consequently, sometimes we are better off living away from one another than with one another.

The problem enters into our thinking when the church puts a higher standard on what God says is lawful than it puts on God Himself. Divorce, as ugly as it is, is not the end of life. It is the end of a marriage. It is the change of a family unit, and for some it is the death of that family unit. It is a detour that was neither expected nor desired—but it happened, and life is more than "divorce." Some family units find new ways to exist, just in an altered state. It is not the preferred way, but it is a way.

I have a great, spunky friend who is divorced. It was not her choice. She didn't want it, nor did she seek it, but she is divorced. Her children live with her, and she is raising them on a meager income while she goes to school and works to try to provide for their future. She was always a stay-at-home mom, and she loved her role as a mother and, for the most part, as a wife. Her husband, on the other hand, decided that he wanted out. He left, her life changed, and so did the lives of their children—but it was not the end. They are not any less of a family, nor is there any less love among them because one person, the dad, decided to bail out. Now, it is true that the problems may be a little more complex, but she and her children are whole, functioning people, and surprisingly, they are learning to trust God in new and creative ways. They are growing in their faith and in their maturity as people.

That is why she is so disturbed by the message of the Christian community to the divorced. She will frequently say that she is tired of listening to Christian programming on radio that makes a point of emphasizing that a family that is divorced is a nonfamily. She says it is very hard to be with her children and hear someone who is not divorced say that God hates divorce, telling her and her children that they are broken and damaged beyond repair. This may never be said directly, but the somber message is "Divorce is the end."

That is a myth. Just as paralysis is not the end, diabetes is not the end, joblessness is not the end, even homelessness is not the end. Divorce is not the end. No one would prefer it, but if it is part of your life, you are not a branded person because of it. Others may put you into a category and try to keep you there, but emotionally you can refuse to wear a scarlet D.

YOU CAN GO ON

Remember, it is not what happens to you but what you think about what happens to you that counts. If you see yourself as a victim, as a "less than" person who can never have a voice, that is what you will be. The fact that you are divorced will always be sad and you may not want everyone to look at your scar (know what it was all about), but you can go on.

Several years ago I was on a radio program answering questions about difficulties in marriage. A soft-spoken woman said, "I have been in an abusive situation for about twelve years. I know I need to do something but I don't know what to do. Can you help me?" Well, obviously, with the limitations of radio, I couldn't tell her a lot, but when I found out that she lived close enough to make an appointment and come to see me at my office, I was thrilled.

When she showed up, I saw a meek, neatly dressed woman who was concerned about her children but fearful of doing anything wrong. She was a hard worker who had a good job and could support her children and herself if she got away. We talked about the situation and worked out a plan for her to leave. She chose a time when it would be the least traumatic for the children and when she would have enough time to get her things and go without being detected.

She needed to wait a month or so to put aside some extra money, so during that time she prayed, planned, and finally made her move. I was so proud of her! Soon she was out, and she and the children have been living separately ever since. All three are flourishing and doing well. The father was not pleased, of course, but the whole dynamic of family interaction has changed. The children are more secure, the mom is more secure and, strangely, even the dad has found a way of relating to the family without abuse. He is still at odds with the mother, but he realizes that she will not just take without objection whatever he dishes out.

Obviously, it would have been better if they could have worked it out under the same roof. They couldn't, or wouldn't, and so the choice that the mother made was for the well-being of her children, who now are flourishing.

I realize that talking about this topic creates uneasiness. It is almost too scary to mention. I wouldn't want anyone to think that because I am addressing this issue that I am a proponent of divorce. I am not. I have worked tirelessly with many couples, trying to help them work out whatever it takes to stay together. I know why God hates divorce. I hate it, too, but sometimes that's what happens despite everyone's best efforts. Sometimes I feel like the disciples must have felt after hearing Jesus' teaching on divorce. They asked, "If that's the way it's going to be, wouldn't it be better not to marry?" (see Matthew 19:10). I think that is the reason many people choose to live together instead of facing the trauma of a marriage gone bad. It is so hard.

UNTHINKING JUDGMENT

One of the responses I have seen from the church (in many areas) to the divorce situation is judgment. One of the most precious women I know, a woman with a heart for God that beats almost in sync with His, was forced to move out of a marital situation. Her husband's behavior became increasingly bizarre. When she remarried after the death of her first husband, she immediately realized the man she thought she knew was a different person. Her children were affected, and so was she. No amount of counsel or reasoning or prayer changed the situation. So her sad, final choice was to leave, which she did. Her children began to flourish, and for the first time in years she was living as a truly adult woman. She had no intention of remarriage, and she did not seek a divorce. She just knew that living under the same roof with her husband was detrimental to her children and to herself.

In walking through this experience with her, it was amazing to see the number of Sanhedrin-like meetings that were held for her to explain herself, be lectured at, be told what she needed to do. Amazingly, her husband was not treated the same way. He had some meetings, but they were always for the sake of consolation since she was the one who had left. He never had to appear before the court for his behavior. It was as if the greater crime was recognizing the problem and doing something about it rather than being the one who was actually *acting* in the irreconcilable way. Yes, God does hate divorce, but it is not the end and it is not the unforgivable sin.

IT DOESN'T ALWAYS TAKE TWO TO DIVORCE

There are so many myths that attach themselves to the divorce question, no wonder we are in such pain. One of those is the myth that it takes two to divorce. That is not always true. You can want the marriage to stay together and work to keep it together, but if your mate wants out, there is nothing you can do. Then to be told by someone who doesn't know the situation and hasn't lived in your house that it always takes two to make a divorce is sad and condemning. It is making the innocent party a part of the problem. How so? Maybe the innocent person is only guilty of having put up with too much for too long. Can you say that contributed to the breakup when the hope and the prayer was that the marriage would survive?

I truly believe we need to offer a hand of hope to those who are going through the process. The agony is great, but it is not the end of the road.

I have never been divorced. As far as I know, my marriage of thirty-three years is intact. That is not said with any pride. It is only the grace of God that has made the journey possible. Although I haven't been divorced, my heart is saddened for those who have been and who are made to feel that they will be broken for the rest of their lives. That is a myth. It is possible to heal even from a divorce you didn't cause, didn't want, and protested every step of the way. Sometimes there are areas of life you just cannot control.

FOCUSING ON WHAT GOD IS DOING

As we do in all our other human failings, we spend too much time focusing on the problem instead of focusing on what God is doing. What is He teaching? How is He growing you up beyond where you are? If we make marriage an idol and divorce a curse, where does God fit into all of this? I love Jesus' attitude when he met the woman at the well as recorded in John 4:5–29. Step back into the shadows and watch what happened on that hot day so long ago:

So He came to a city of Samaria called Sychar, near the parcel of ground that Jacob gave to his son Joseph; and Jacob's well was there. So Jesus, being wearied from His journey, was sitting thus by the well. It was about the sixth hour.

There came a woman of Samaria to draw water. Jesus said to her, "Give Me a drink." For His disciples had gone away into the city to buy food. Therefore the Samaritan woman said to Him, "How is it that You, being a Jew, ask me for a drink since I am a Samaritan woman?" (For Jews have no dealings with Samaritans.) Jesus answered and said to her, "If you knew the gift of God, and who it is who says to you, 'Give Me a drink,' you would have asked Him, and He would have given you living water." She said to Him, "Sir, You have nothing to draw with and the well is deep; where then do You get that living water? You are not greater than our father Jacob, are You, who gave us the well, and drank of it himself and his sons and his cattle?" Jesus answered and said to her, "Everyone who drinks of this water will thirst again; but whoever drinks of the water that I will give him shall never thirst; but the water that I will give him will become in him a well of water springing up to eternal life."

The woman said to Him, "Sir, give me this water, so I will not be thirsty nor come all the way here to draw." He said to her, "Go, call your husband and come here." The woman answered and said, "I have no husband." Jesus said to her, "You have correctly said, 'I have no husband'; for you have had five husbands, and the one whom you now have is not your husband; this you have said truly." The woman said to Him, "Sir, I perceive that You are a prophet. Our fathers worshiped in this mountain, and you people say that in Jerusalem is the place where men ought to worship." Jesus said to her, "Woman, believe Me, an hour is coming when neither in this mountain nor in Jerusalem will you worship the Father. You worship what you do not know; we worship what we know, for salvation is from the Jews. But an hour is coming, and now is, when the true worshipers will worship the Father in spirit and truth; for such people the Father seeks to be His worshipers. God is spirit, and those who worship Him must worship in spirit and truth." The woman said to Him, "I know that Messiah is coming (He who is called Christ); when that One comes, He will declare all things to us." Jesus said to her, "I who speak to you am He."

At this point His disciples came, and they were amazed that He had been speaking with a woman, yet no one said, "What do You seek?" or, "Why do You speak with her?" So the woman left her waterpot, and went into the city and said to the men, "Come, see a man who told me all the things that I have done; this is not the Christ, is it?"

Jesus had met quite a woman. From verse 28, it is obvious that she knew how to communicate with a man. After her encounter with Jesus, it is recorded, "So the woman left her waterpot, and went into the city and said to the men . . ." She went back to town and began talking to the men. Whether these were ex-husbands, her boyfriend and his friends, or just the men of the village, we don't know. But she had found what she needed, and she wanted everyone to find the same thing.

Pseudorelationships, multiple marriages, and feel-good situations never satisfy. Judgment, shame, criticism, and rejection never correct. Jesus is the only One who can speak peace to a troubled heart. So that is where the focus has to be.

THE FREEDOM OF FORGIVENESS

The truth of divorce is that because of someone's hardened heart, the marriage is in a mess. That is what divorce indicates. Whether you are the one who has experienced the hardened heart of one you love and, therefore, you are divorced against your will, or whether you are the one whose heart was hard and you are living with the regrets, divorce is still not the end.

No matter what your situation is, truth will bring freedom to your life.

Since there is no sin God cannot forgive, even if you have created the messiest mess of all, you can know the freedom of being forgiven.

> *If we say that we have fellowship with Him and yet walk in the darkness, we lie and do not practice the truth; but if we walk in the Light as He Himself is in the Light, we have fellowship with one another, and the blood of Jesus His Son cleanses us from all sin. If we say that we have no sin, we are deceiving ourselves and the truth is not in us. If we confess our sins, He is faithful and righteous to forgive us our sins and to cleanse us from all unrighteousness.* (1 JOHN 1:6–9)

If you have been cleansed from all unrighteousness, you are free of wearing the mark of one who has sinned. No more scarlet Ds. You may have to face uncomfortable circumstances—that is life. You don't have to be branded and condemned because you have committed the unpardonable sin.

HEALING

On the Internet there is a wonderful Web site called Broken Circle. It offers warm, caring, biblical advice and compassion for people going through divorce. I thought the following information was timely and helpful for anyone who has believed that divorce is the end. It answers a critical question.

HOW CAN A CHRISTIAN BEGIN TO HEAL?

I know when I first accepted the fact that my marriage was over and I would have to begin again, I wondered how much time I needed to heal. This is a fundamental question we all ask because as terrifying as divorce is, we want to be able to move away from the pain and reclaim life. Old sayings are generally true, such as "Each person heals at a different speed" and "Time can be a friend."

But healing for a person who has a relationship with Christ should be fundamentally different than the world's standards. This does not mean that it happens faster or easier, but a Christian who will completely give himself or herself to . . . God's care will be able to see the spiritual dynamic that exists in all situations both good and bad.

I personally feel that the word "divorce" is too kind a term. I prefer to think of it as "the death of a family." Our society has become numb to what divorce actually is. I also feel that divorce is more difficult to heal from than the death of a spouse because of the broken dreams, promises, and the feelings of betrayal. These are not easy to simply lay aside.

Unfortunately, I cannot offer you a twelve step program to healing from a divorce. Each person is different and each person will heal from a tragedy in a different way. I believe God knows this about us and he helps in different ways, so what I would like to do is share some fundamental things that have helped me and the others who consult with me for the content in this site.

1. You, no doubt, will feel many different emotions. Common ones are depression, sadness, anger, guilt, instability, and even a sense that life

has ended. These feelings are normal. I found that when I had days where I was very depressed or angry, I would simply tell myself, "These feelings are normal and okay." Sometimes I think we try very hard to make ourselves feel better when in fact we need to give ourselves time to grieve. You will find that these feelings come and go and often return days and months down the road without any provocation. This too is normal. In a nutshell, you are a human; allow yourself to be one and allow yourself to feel the grief.

2. Although these human feelings are normal, I learned a key to gaining great insight and peace when my divorce first began. I have relied on this time and time again, but it does not come easily or lightly. My daughter was only fourteen months old when my ex-wife decided to leave me. Thinking about the future for my daughter in a broken home was almost dizzying. I cried out to God for help—I cried to God and told Him what he should do! But God began to teach me that I could not control the situation. In fact, it was totally out of my control. This was an important turning point. All too often, we seek to control the situations in our lives, when in fact, very few situations are actually in our control. This is when I began to see that many things were coming I could not control, but I could control myself—I could control my responses, and I could control how much of myself I turned over to God. Here is what I did:

A. I first released myself to God. I stopped trying to be the one in control and prayed a simple prayer asking God to completely take over and give me the wisdom to simply follow Him. This is not a prayer you can half say and expect God to work—He sees your heart. But when you totally give yourself over to Him, then He can begin to work.

B. I next asked God to give me spiritual sight—in other words, help me catch a glimpse of how He sees the situation. When I did this, I began to see "outside" of myself. I began to see the brokenness God felt as well. I felt his Spirit begin to correct my thoughts as I constantly sought His face—the peace was overwhelming. This peace did not correct the situation, but peace is not the absence of suffering, but it truly is the presence of God.

C. I was heartbroken over my marriage, but extremely depressed about my child. Then in simple prayer one day, God reminded me that He loves my child more than I do, and He is watching over her. A simple idea, yet profound.

These things began to heal me, they began to show me a bigger picture outside of myself. For when I truly stepped away from the tragedy and simply tried to "hide" behind God, He worked in a powerful way. HE WILL BE FOUND FOR THOSE WHO TRULY SEEK HIS FACE.

3. Don't do anything without prayer. Child custody issues, settlements, divorce suits, and all of the other things that come can be blinding. I found that taking a passive position helped. This does not mean that you do not take action, but it means that for every situation that demands action, you pray first and ask God how to handle the situation.

4. Try to take things one day at a time. No one, except God, knows what tomorrow will bring anyway. Try to handle the problems of the day and not spend time worrying about tomorrow.

5. Ironically, the death of your family puts you in a distinct position to spend a great amount of time growing your relationship with God. Divorce is never what God wants for a family, but through pain and tragedy, God can grow your faith in Him in a way you might not . . . even imagine. I know!

6. Is the divorce primarily your fault? Seek forgiveness and then seek forgiveness from your spouse. Even if the relationship cannot be saved, you have the responsibility to God and your spouse to seek forgiveness.

7. This one may seem difficult, especially if you are experiencing a lot of anger, but you need to pray for your ex-wife/ex-husband. You do have to come to a point where you release that person to God's care and ask Him to do a work in his/her life.

8. Finally, give yourself a break. Let others help you. Do things you enjoy and that relax you. Sleep, eat well-balanced meals, and take care of your physical body. Entrust your spiritual well being to God and take care of yourself. If you need to cry, cry. If you feel sad, that's okay. When you begin to feel happy, let yourself. Most importantly, don't keep this bottled up inside. You need to talk it out. Let your friends and family help you, seek a Christian support group. . . .

As for those of you who are just beginning, remember that divorce is like following a small trail through the woods blindfolded. The way can be uncertain, so it's best to hold the hand of the One who already knows the way.[1]

GOD LOVES YOU

If you have bought into the myth that divorce is the end and you are damaged beyond repair, take courage. God hates divorce, but He loves you. He hates the fact you and those around you have been hurt by divorce. No one wins, and everyone is affected. God's heart is always reconciliation, but God is not a taskmaster expecting you to "make bricks without straw." That's how the Egyptians treated the children of Israel. They wanted to give them a task too big to accomplish without the means to accomplish it. They knew that would be totally demoralizing.

That is not God's heart, nor is that His assignment for you. Others may condemn you and tell you that it is over—that you no longer are usable or even desirable for service to God. Don't believe it for a minute. I would have to bring up our favorite question, "Where is it written?" If your "ex" won't reconcile, so be it. You have a Lover of your soul who is longing to take you on a journey, a journey including plans for a future and a hope.

THE MYTH
OF
EVERYTHING
IS AS IT SEEMS

There is an adult reality we must all face. *Life is what you make it.* Let me say that again. *Life is what you make it.* Once that truth dawns on you, then the myth of "everything is as it seems" will become a hazy glow from the past.

There are those who would try to convince you that your life consists of what you were given at birth. Others would say, "No, it's what happens to you along the way." Still others would say that it is both your genetics and your environment that matter. Clearly both play a part in your life, but they cannot determine your success or failure as a person. If you believe they do, then if you were genetically short-changed, life is "less than" for you. You are automatically at a disadvantage. Others are better looking, more intelligent, funnier, and have more pleasant personalities.

I mean, *look* at Cinderella. We remember her as beautiful, and her poor old stepsisters always will be remembered as ugly. They didn't have what Cinderella had, so, although she had to do hard chores, her beauty was what got her through. No prince was going to come along to get the stepsisters out of their low estate. They were ugly, and they had to make it the best way they could—which in their case was to be overbearing and mean. It is natural to see someone who has been endowed with natural beauty and believe that they will come up in a better situation than anyone else. (The reality is that attractive people do have some advantages in the beginning, but they do not maintain a head start forever.) But remember, everything is not as it seems.

Beauty and the breaks in life are believed to play a huge role in success. If you have family money, athletic skills, or high intelligence, it should follow as night follows day that you should be successful. You have been lavishly loved and coddled by doting parents. You should soar. Yet we all know that environment doesn't necessarily make wonderful things happen. Sometimes beautiful people, smart people, and wealthy people are miserable. They curse the very thing that others would say is their advantage. They even say, "I wish I were like everybody else. I wouldn't be miserable."

IT'S NOT WHAT HAPPENS BUT WHAT YOU THINK ABOUT WHAT HAPPENS

The truth is that *the way you view your life is the biggest determinate of your success.* This has been established in psychological circles for years. The statement that a good practitioner will use repeatedly is, "It's not what happens to you that matters, but what you think about what happens to you." That is a truth that was established by God—in the Proverbs thousands of years ago, "As a man thinks, so he is" (see Proverbs 23:7).

Thoughts rule! What you think drives your emotions. What you think causes you to behave the way you behave. Your thinking is a product of your own choice, of what you have been taught, and of how you process what you hear. In other words, you are in control of your perceptions. You can't change what you have been taught, but you can question it. You can't change what is said to you, but you can determine how or if you will take it in. You can choose what to think about all of it. We all have a filter through which we process everything that happens. So when an event occurs, it comes to you through *your* filter. That is the only way it can get to you. It has to pass through your grid. That is why the filter is so important.

Let's say that your best friend decides that she is no longer your best friend. I know that sounds like junior high school, but let's face it—most of us at one time or another have had a best friend move away, walk away, or emotionally disappear. The effect of such an event on your life is *up to you.* You can see it as the most awful thing that can happen. You can see it as a chance for your friend to have new opportunities for growth. You can see it as a time for you to grow in a new way. You can be mad at God for letting your best friend walk away. You can become defensive and announce that you got along without her before you met her and you can get along without her now. Each of these responses is a choice—*choices that you can make of your own free will.*

Now others may tell you what they think about your best friend's not being around anymore. Some will perceive your response as sadness and will be sympathetic to your pain. Some will be angry that you have been left and will take up your sense of offense (that you may or may not have). Some will analyze the situation and explain to you that the relationship was unhealthy for a long time, so you are better off. Some will say, "You know it takes two for this kind of thing to happen, so you might want to check yourself for what you have done that has caused this." If you depended on everyone else's opinion, you could be confused—and stay confused, wondering, "What is the truth here?"

YOUR GRID DETERMINES HOW YOU INTERPRET THE TRUTH

What you must understand is that if you want to know the truth, you have to look for it and accept it when you find it. You have to recognize that you have a filter. It is up to you to make sure that it is a clean, clear filter that will allow truth to get through. If you want to live in truth and experience the benefits of truth, you will need to be able to recognize truth when you see it. Questioning that is earnest and open will allow you to see the truth as it is, not as you perceive it.

The New Testament definition of truth is based on the word *aletheia.* It means the unveiled reality lying at the basis of an appearance. It means the reality clearly lying before our eyes as opposed to a mere appearance.

Work must be done if we want to know truth. We have to "unveil" the reality beneath the appearance. Doing that takes a thoughtful assessment of the facts, and it takes time. That is why things look so different in the morning and why it is good never to make a decision when you are tired or hungry. Your filter is influenced by your physical situation.

When we hear or see something, many of us immediately form an opinion based on our grid. That opinion may or may not be factual, but more than likely this initial opinion is what will stick with us as we process events surrounding what we have heard or seen.

A case in point is the Elian Gonzalez case. The small Cuban boy was rescued from the ocean by a fisherman. His mom had died trying to escape from Cuba with him. It was obvious that she desired freedom in America for herself and her son. But he alone survived. The furor that followed his rescue from the ocean had so many layers of truth, perception, and distortion entwined with high emotion that it was almost impossible to get a handle on what really was true and, therefore, what was the best action to take in regard to the surviving boy.

Americans were polarized. If you stood back and looked at it, this was the perfect picture of "everything is not as it seems." Some saw the Miami relatives who were taking care of the boy as the most loving situation for him to grow up in. For the most part, their supporters were Cuban exiles who had risked their lives for a life in America. Their grid was freedom at all costs.

Then there was his father, who had been left behind in Cuba and was now his only parent. Those who supported the father's claims saw the parental bond as the most important issue. They put themselves in the father's shoes: Every father should be with his son.

Other Cuban exiles focused on the picture of the INS agent, dressed in riot gear, holding a gun, and taking the boy away from his Miami relatives by dark of night. That picture brought terror or comfort, depending on the grid through which it was viewed.

Seeing Elian being whisked away and put into a car with strangers revived old feelings of terror some of the Cuban exiles had experienced when they were forced to leave their homes at night to escape danger.

For others, the picture of Elian reunited with his dad elicited feelings of joy. Being with a father meant comfort to them. Still others feared what really was going on behind closed doors. Memories of a father brought pain to them. So, you see, everything is not as it seems because each of us has a filter through which we process information.

In his book *Life Strategies,* Phil McGraw writes, "Because you are a unique individual, your perceptions are unique. No matter how much you think you are like another person, the meanings you assign to what takes place in your life are yours alone. The failure to recognize this principle has created more trouble than you could ever imagine."[1]

As Christians, we are different from one another. We think and feel differently and we relate to God and one another in a different way. We are from different cultures and different backgrounds. We have been taught by different teachers and indoctrinated into the dogma of different churches. We relate to God and one another differently—but we are still part of the family of God through faith in the work of the Lord Jesus Christ. That is our unity. For some of us that is not enough, so we try to fit into what is currently thought to be spiritual. We do that so we can be accepted and feel good about our Christianity. The problem is that not every passing trend fits who we are as individuals, and as a result there is a lot of frustration and self-doubt.

Twenty years ago, when I had children at home, I had never heard of home schooling and Christian schools were not in vogue. They were in existence, just not in vogue. My boys attended public school, had great teachers, and thrived under their tutelage. During that period I had an experience that disturbed me then and rankles my emotions even now. Just thinking about it makes me want to scream, "Where is it written?" (If I had to relive this event, no doubt I would ask that very question, but nonetheless, this is what happened.)

My youngest son and I were traveling on an airliner together. We had had a great mother-son trip and were returning home with good memories and good feelings. The man who shared the row of seats with us engaged me in conversation, since I was sitting between him and my son. He asked where we lived and where we went to church. Eventually he got around to asking where my son went to school. I told him, "The public school." At that point the man (who I later found out was a pastor) began to tell me what was going to happen to my child because we didn't have him enrolled in a Christian school. He finished his speech by telling me that my son would "grow up to spit in [my] face."

Obviously, this was his opinion, but it was not truth. He had a belief based on who knows what, and he was appalled that my belief was different. (I would like to report that my son, who is now twenty-five, has yet to spit in my face. He is a fine Christian husband and father who loves the Lord and faithfully serves in his church.)

I have been a Christian for thirty years. In that time, I have seen waves of "spirituality" float through our Christian circles. It has been so interesting to see emotions ripple when people try to fit into the "molds." When home schooling first came out, tensions surfaced between the home schoolers and the public schoolers. Why? Because each group thought it had the truth. But this was not a truth issue. It was a preference issue. Unfortunately, the fear of being thought unspiritual has caused many of us to behave in ways that are no more authentic than a bunch of plastic flowers.

Tossing around ought tos and shoulds does nothing but create bondage. There are those who believe in birth control and those who don't. Who is right? There are those who believe a woman can work outside the home and care for her children. There are those who think that any woman who does that loves money more than her children. Who is right? There are those who believe that a woman's head should be covered, and there are those who believe that idea is a throwback to the Law. Who is right?

What happens when we meet these issues? We experience confusion and often feel as if we fall short. Before I understood the truth that each of us can hold his own convictions (Romans 14), I used to feel terribly unspiritual when my neighbor came over unannounced. She did not believe in television. I did. If I knew she was coming, I turned off the TV out of respect for her. If I didn't know she was coming, I was uncomfortable when she walked in the door and felt very unclean until I could get the thing turned off. Who was right? Neither. We both just had differing convictions.

Until you understand that we are different and that is OK, it is easy to feel less than spiritual when those differences come up. The key to finding peace is settling the issues for *yourself* by asking, "Where is it written?" If you don't ask this question you will end up thinking that you fall short. Then it is easy to slip into some pious platitude and pretend for others that is the way you really live your life. Of course, you know all along that you really don't live that way. You think it is probably true for someone who is more spiritual, but it just doesn't work for you.

How many times have I heard the well-worn *J* (Jesus first), *O* (Others second), *Y* (You third)? That has a pretty ring to it, but who on earth lives that way? I don't know anyone who does. Life is too fluid, too changeable. At times it can be Jesus first (I guess; but now that I think about it, what does that mean?). Every hour of the day we are responding to life, and whoever comes to the top of the heap is the one who gets the most attention. Since it is Jesus who says, "I will never leave you nor forsake you," it really isn't a matter of putting Him first. He is already first. It is a matter of acknowledging Him as your life. Then everything else falls into place. That is all you can do.

It is a myth to think that you can compartmentalize life into a religious formula. Life happens, and we have to respond to it as it happens. So our response cannot be from a formula. It must come from the Life that is in us. It is Christ who lives His life through us as we give up and realize that our formulas look good on framed prints but hold no intrinsic power. The need of our lives is for a *relationship with God.* It is how we look through our circumstantial filter to the essence of what life is about.

A WOMAN WITH A PROBLEM

A certain woman in Scripture is particularly interesting to me. She had a problem, and she believed she knew who could fix it. When she encountered the Lord, she made no pretense of the fact that her problem was the paramount issue in her life. Her problem was the grid through which she saw life. Read what the gospel writer Mark records about her situation. Note that her problem was not only her grid for seeing the world but the world's grid for seeing her. She was known as the bleeding woman. That twelve-year hemorrhage defined who she was.

A woman who had had a hemorrhage for twelve years, and had endured much at the hands many physicians, and had spent all that she had and was not helped at all, but rather had grown worse . . . [She knew she was getting no better despite her best efforts and the physician's opinion!] [A]fter hearing about Jesus, she came up in the crowd behind Him and touched His cloak. For she thought, "If I just touch His garments, I will get well." [She had decided what she needed to do, and she did it! The rest is history; recorded for all time!] Immediately the flow of her blood was dried up; and she felt in her body that she was healed of her affliction. Immediately Jesus, perceiving in Himself that the power proceeding from Him had gone forth, turned around in the crowd and said, "Who touched My garments?" And His disciples said to Him, "You see the crowd pressing in on You, and You say, 'Who touched Me?'" And He looked around to see the woman who had done this. But the woman fearing and trembling, aware of what had happened to her, came and fell down before Him and told Him the whole truth. And He said to her, "Daughter, your faith has made you well; go in peace and be healed of your affliction." (MARK 5:25–34)

Whatever the problem might be, if you are suffering, there are great principles to think about here. They all have to do with the myth of things are not as they seem.

The woman had tried the conventional route to deal with her problem. The wisdom we usually run on is to do the logical, sane, safe thing when we encounter a difficulty. For her, it was to seek the advice of the physicians, the experts. It would seem that they could have healed her after all that time—but she was not going to be healed by the physicians. Obviously, there was another plan. But what was it? She needed something else, but she didn't even know what it was.

That is so often where we find ourselves. How many times has it occurred to me that I need something else? How many times have I found it in a place I didn't even know existed? Being willing to look outside your comfort zone can be the most glorious first step you can take toward healthy change. It is the very first step toward totally debunking the myth that everything is as it seems.

This Gentile woman came to a point where she was willing to do something radical and scary. She would look for and she would find Jesus. If she could just get to Him, surely she could be healed. She got only close enough to Him to touch the hem of His garment, but she was healed. Case closed?

Well, not exactly. Jesus had some business He wanted to attend to. "Who touched me?" He asked.

The disciples, always ready to give a good explanation, said, "Please. Look at this crowd. Fifteen of them have touched you in the last minute alone and you want to know, 'Who touched Me?'"

Things are not always as they seem.

Jesus, as usual, didn't stop to discuss their small-mindedness. He just zeroed in on the object of His affection. He saw the woman.

This was the moment of truth for her.

She and Jesus would talk about things as they were, not things as someone might perceive them.

She fell down before Him and told Him the whole truth. Although she was frightened, she didn't say, "Oh, I'm sorry. I didn't mean to touch you."

She didn't look around and say, "I am so sorry that I interrupted your healing service. I know there's a dead child who needs you more" (see Mark 5:35–36).

She just knew that she needed Jesus.

Now, that is a perception that is always true. If you are needy in any way, you need Jesus. Moreover, He is involved in everything that involves you. I think the point to be made here is that there is always the conventional way to do things, but that doesn't always work. It is what you try first, but when there are no answers, you can get radical— look for Jesus.

We women need this message more than anything because we usually like to keep to the rules. That brings acceptance and approval most of the time. But does it bring about the radical change and healing we all long for in our lives? Because of the myth that everything there is as it seems, there is all the more reason to ask, "Where is it written?"

> *There is a way which seems right to a man,*
> *But its end is the way of death.*
> *Even in laughter the heart may be in pain,*
> *And the end of joy may be grief.*
> (PROVERBS 14:12–13)

If you are ever going to grow, change, and find what God has for you in Christ, you have to seek for it without restricting what He can show you. Your grid may tell you that Jesus can only act in a certain way. When He acts another way, you may wonder, "What was that? Was that a coincidence or a fluke or what?" Since Jesus is supreme and able to do whatever He wants, He is under no obligation to act in restricted ways. We are the ones under obligation. We, my dear sisters, are obligated to keep on seeking, keep on asking, keep on knocking. We are obligated to question ourselves because our personal grids are like traps in which the truth can become tangled. We need to know ourselves and our tendencies. We need to ask ourselves, "How do I usually see events?" That is one of the best ways to avoid getting caught up in some stifling myth.

COGNITIVE ERRORS

In the book *Telling the Truth to Troubled People,* William Backus quotes A. T. Beck's description of major cognitive errors and how they are generated. Backus says, "If you will look at [these cognitive errors], you will see they are common chinks in the armor of faith through which the fiery darts of the enemy can travel to pierce us where it hurts."[2] If you carefully study these errors, you will be able to hear yourself and straighten your grid before you get into a mythical mess.

Cognitive Error #1: Selective abstraction. Here the sufferer is focused only on certain details from a complex picture, using just those details to describe the entire experience.[3]

Let's say that you are in a group of women at your office, and they go to lunch but fail to ask you to join them. There has been no problem and you work well together, but on this day they just don't ask you to join them. *Selective abstraction* makes an assumption that they don't like you; therefore, they didn't invite you; therefore, you are unlovable. Never mind that you have had pleasant experiences all day.

Take it a little further to your relationship with the Lord. You have prayed for Him to give you a new job, but your request has been denied. Your feeling is that He doesn't find you worthy of the answer you wanted; therefore, you feel estranged from Him. *Selective abstraction* focuses on the negative in any situation and uses it to feed any negative belief that you might have. If you already think you are unlovable, *selective abstraction* just proves it.

Cognitive Error #2: Arbitrary inference. This is drawing a conclusion without evidence, or in the face of evidence to the contrary. "I know my next performance evaluation is going to be so bad I may lose my job," said Eleanor. Further questioning revealed that no one had reprimanded Eleanor at all over the period for which she was to be evaluated. "That's just it. They haven't said anything. I think they are saving it all for the review session." Eleanor reasoned in a purely arbitrary fashion. Notice that by this method she was able to argue from the *lack of criticism* that she was full of faults![4]

Cognitive Error #3: Overgeneralization. Drawing a conclusion on the basis of a single incident.[5]

When Harriet came home and her kitchen sink was stopped up, she called her husband and told him the whole house was falling apart. He needed to come home and do something about it! (This error is really a pretty common myth-maker.)

Cognitive Error #4: Personalization. This error involves relating events to oneself without clear evidence that they are so related. "The Joneses went home early, and I know it's because they can't stand me when I'm this way. I'm so repulsive it's a wonder they came at all!" Jane wailed. Questioning revealed that the Joneses stayed through a fairly long evening, did not go home until 11:30 P.M., and spoke repeatedly to Jane of the wonderful time they had visiting with her. Yet Jane was able to conclude that the Joneses departed because they disliked her personality![6]

Cognitive Error #5: Dichotomous thinking. Classifying either/or or all/none categories when they really can be better understood as existing on a continuum. This misbelief device is very commonly used by [many women] to put themselves down. Thus, if [you are] not perfect, [you are] awful. [If you are not beautiful, then you are ugly. If you aren't at the top, you are the bottom.] If things don't go precisely as planned, they are hopelessly out of control.[7]

Can you take this information and use it to question your thinking? It is amazing when you actually turn up your internal dialogue so that you can hear it. If you listen to yourself and hear any one of these cognitive errors coming from your mouth, then you have a major insight into the myth that everything is as it seems. The fact that something appears to be true through your grid does not necessarily make it true.

FRIENDS WHO CAN HELP YOU SEE THE TRUTH

The first check is to ask yourself, "Where is it written?"

We know this already. This one question will eliminate a lot if you are really willing to get into the Word and dig out what God says about Himself and His instructions about how you are to treat others.

Occasionally, you may be up against a knotty situation that has you stumped no matter how much you look for it in the Book. This is where a group of people to whom you are willing to be accountable and vulnerable is important. We all have friends, but our friends don't always call us on our faulty thinking unless they are mature and the friendship is very secure. A group that agrees to speak the truth and continues to love, no matter what, is a safeguard against being duped by the myth that everything is as it seems.

For several years I have met with a wonderful group of women on a regular basis. They are very different in their backgrounds, ages, and interests, but they all have an intense desire to grow. They have covenanted together to tell each other the truth, to be scrupulous in confidentiality, and to encourage one another to grow. It has been wonderful to see the grid-straightening that has gone on.

If you are miserable because you live in the fog of not knowing what reality is in your life, then the big girl thing to do is keep going until you find out what you are believing that is causing you grief. The little woman will retreat to her heap, believe that everything she thinks is the truth, and that the rest of the world is wrong.

A group of women in another state has met together for the purpose of mutual accountability and growth. They have tackled some of these issues by challenging their thinking, determining what needs to be changed in the way they are thinking, and replacing the faulty part of their thinking with fresh truth.

Here is a report from the meeting where they were challenging their existing beliefs about being little women. These women were given the assignment to go home and ask their husbands what they believed about the role of wives. I've changed the names for their protection, but the comments are the same as reported by the leader.

- Eleanor's husband said his code for a "good wife" was one who kept the house (or hired it done) and the yard, looked good, kept her weight in balance, stayed fit, played golf when he needed a partner, cooked meals, was a good hostess, gave the best parties, kept their social network going, decorated the house for every season, paid all the bills, had a good sense of business, was well-informed regarding international affairs, could converse well when called upon, was a mom who produced great children, and provided great sex!

  Since Eleanor began meeting with her accountability group, she has challenged some of her thoughts and has replaced them with truth. Believing the truth and acting on it has caused a change in her behavior.

  Eleanor's husband has changed also. He is now ironing his own sport shirts, taking his own clothes to the cleaners, and picking them up, because he is *so* picky. Her belief in the truth, not just an acquiescence to a superimposed code, has brought about many significant attitudinal changes. When they discussed his point of view, they both laughed at how ludicrous his old viewpoint had been.

  Attitudinal change has more opportunity when it is bathed in the clear light of truth. If you are caught in some sort of web of believing that everything is as it seems, then you will be trapped (I really should say doomed) into doing what you have always done, in the same way, and with grossly disappointing results.

- Lydia said that her husband married her so that he would have someone to adore him, and she married him for security. She said that they had agreed that she would no longer adore him, but would love him honestly and authentically, and confront and challenge him as she grew up and became herself. He agreed to this plan, but said that he was afraid he was just too old (sixty-two) to change. She told him that he would simply have to find a way to do it because their old pattern had been discarded. It is the right thing to do. He *is* doing it and likes it.

- Betty resigned as the Social Director of their family. When her children called and wanted to know what *she* was planning for their grandmother's birthday, she told them that she and her husband were taking Grandmother to dinner on Friday night . . . and that they, the children, would need to figure out what *they* wanted to do for her. She's out of the hub—*and* resigned as her eighty-year-old mother's "little girl." Everything is changing at her house. She has recognized the myth, worked it through practically, and replaced it with the truth.

The leader of the group commented, "These women are transitioning wisely and well. We determined that a lot of our relationships had really been buying-and-selling—not genuine loving. They had little to do with Jesus or the gospel . . . and much of it would be burned up . . . a *lot* of family dinners, trips, and parties would be tossed onto the fire!"

Paul was writing to the Corinthian believers who were immature and in need of much growth when he wrote:

> *Each man's work will become evident; for the day will show it because it is to be revealed with fire, and the fire itself will test the quality of each man's work. If any man's work which he has built on it remains, he will receive a reward. If any man's work is burned up, he will suffer loss; but he himself will be saved, yet so as through fire.* (1 CORINTHIANS 3:13–15)

Are you beginning to see that everything is not as it seems? Do you see the necessity of doing some work to dig out the truth and find a way to authentically incorporate it into your life? Hanging on to the myth of everything is as it seems will leave you stuck in a trap that will keep you from the greatness of life and bigness of spirit God intends for you.

Let's be clear about what you're hunting for. Beliefs are things you hold to be true and accurate. You treat them as fact; you no longer test them, let alone challenge them, because you believe you have found the truth, end of story. . . . You know it is true so you just accept it and live with it.[8]

Do you want to accept it and live with it? What would it take for you to desire to change and do the work you will need to do? Are you willing to risk questioning your own closely held truths? It could change your life forever!

CHAPTER NINE

THE MYTH OF IT'S POSSIBLE TO PLAY WITH FIRE AND NOT BE BURNED

On the surface, this seems like a no-brainer; but when you consider the subtle way Satan made his deadly insinuation to Eve, sometimes I wonder if we really know what fire is! Fire burns—it's hot. It can cause damage before you even know what has happened to you!

I was on one of my yearly cooking binges this past Christmas. I stuck my arm too far into the oven, not once but twice, and months later I still have scars. I only touched the hot rack for a millisecond. I didn't mean to touch it. I thought I could avoid it the second time, but I touched it again. And although the oven has cooled, and whatever was cooking is long forgotten, I have two very obvious scars on my arm! That is often what it's like when we believe we can come close to fire and not be burned.

BRUSHES WITH FIRE HAVE MYTHICAL ROOTS

I am convinced that all our brushes with fire have their roots in those two original myths in the Garden of Eden we have heard so much about: *God's holding out on you, and God doesn't mean what He says.*

In his book *The Hidden Rift with God,* William Backus provides an insightful description that gives the root thinking of what it takes to believe that God is less than who He says He is:

> *God's will for me and His commands are what's best for Him, not for me.* His insistence that I obey Him only springs from a tyrannical heart, or an egotistical need to be in control.
>
> *If God's commands are not best for me, then He must be lying to His own advantage.* He cannot be trusted. I can never be sure God wills the good for me, especially if it appears that my good might diminish Him, or interfere with a plan of His, or limit His control over me.
>
> *Even if God doesn't come right out and lie about the good, He might be wrong about what's good for me.* It doesn't matter whether God lies or simply doesn't know what's good for me as well as I do. I am now in the position of God.
>
> *Therefore, I will have to decide for myself what the good is.* I can't rely on anybody. I'm the only one I can trust. I'm the final arbiter of my own good. The accompanying truth I must now face is terrifying: I am alone and mistakes can be worse than fatal.[1]

This is the thought progression of a person who believes that God is holding out and God doesn't mean what He says.

You may recognize your own thinking here. It is a very common thought process that I have discovered in women who are willing to play too close to the flame.

This is what got my friend Shelly into trouble. She is a lovable, attractive woman. She looks younger than she is. She was very disappointed in her husband, Jim, who is older and far more settled than she. Convinced that she needed to be understood and deserved to have a good time—and believing it wasn't going to happen with Jim, Shelly formed an exciting bond with a younger man in the choir at her church.

They were both solo quality musicians, so they had the opportunity to sing together on several occasions. They were the perfect pair. Shelly began to fantasize about a future with her singing partner. She never told him. She never told Jim. She just played close to the fire. Jim became more and more disgusting to her. She became more and more torn until she was in a complete turmoil. Then she decided she need-ed to take matters into her own hands. Maybe her singing partner would like to have a closer relationship. The younger man liked Shelly, but he wasn't interested in her advances, so soon he began to back away from her. Shelly continued to attend church and be married to Jim, but her brush with the flame had disappointed her and left her depressed. If Jim was so boring to her and if God was holding out on her and didn't mean what He said, what was there in life for her anyway?

Oh, what a common question. Is there life for me? What will it look like, and where is it coming from? God seems so unpredictable and dangerous. How can I relax and trust Him? He is so slow and I want it *now.* If He is so difficult anyway, why don't I just avoid Him and do my own thing? I am saved and I know it. Heaven is waiting for me. Now I have to manage a way to get there without messing up too badly.

FRIENDLY FIRE

One of the areas we don't hear much about in Christian circles is the fire of emotional dependency that burns holes in hearts and mess-es up lives right and left. It starts as a strong emotional seduction that may or may not lead to a sexual involvement. When it does become sexual, it is just one component of the whole package. "Lifestyle" is the term used to describe the full spectrum of experience. So many women caught in the deception have played with fire and found themselves on fire. They are burned, branded, and there aren't many places to turn to find a way out. There are some excellent organizations that have great material, but for the woman caught in a once-in-a-lifetime situation, it is daunting to try to heal from the injury of it all.

There are usually two kinds of situations that cause terror and burn-ing. One is the woman caught in the total deception that she was cre-ated a homosexual and, therefore, this is the only life she can lead. The other is the woman who believes that she needs another woman as a companion and friend or that she is needed as a companion and friend. The need becomes a bondage, and the relationship goes too far. For either category of individual, there is hope and healing. There may not be a lot of understanding or compassion from people who have never been burned by this kind of fire, but Jesus offers hope and healing that defies the Enemy's mythical insinuations.

One of the first steps toward healing is to recognize that you have a problem. If you are in a tumultuous relationship with another woman, then you may need to look at symptoms of a relationship that is too close to the fire. It may not be a full-blown lesbian relationship in nature, but it can surely be emotionally dependent and fraught with peril for both of you.

In *Among Friends,* Letty Cottin Pogrebin writes:

> We want friends we can depend upon, and in turn, we also pride ourselves on being the rock in someone else's storm. But the cloying, draining energy-sucking friend is not a thing of beauty and a joy forever. The ties that bind can also strangle.
>
> Dependency is a suffocating form of enclosure. And weakness can be a powerful tool for manipulation in the hands of the friend who is incessantly needy or inconsolable, the one who keeps escalating the crises that require your intervention, and the one whose daily conversation resounds with cries of "I'm falling apart." However faint the voice, such pleas can be as coercive as a shout.[2]

This is the description of a relationship that starts out with good intentions. Being there for our friends is important. But when "being there" becomes the only way you can relate and you begin to see that you aren't there for others, then you have just walked into a trap. You have moved a little closer to a fire that eventually will consume you.

The subtlety of all this is that it does not look like a sinful relationship. It looks like a person you can help. You believe you can help, you want to help, and you ask yourself, "Isn't true Christianity laying your life down for another person?" If you hear the whine of a voice in the background egging you on to be another woman's all in all, beware. If she depends on you to be her rock, savior, companion, and friend, then you are hearing the voice of the Enemy, who is injecting just enough blinding agent into your field of vision to prevent you from seeing where all of this is leading. You may even feel the warmth of the fire, but because you are partially blinded, you can't see how closely you are moving toward the fire pit.

We all want a payoff of some kind for our investments. Investment in relationships is no different from any other. We want to receive something in return, whether it is acceptance, esteem, love, understanding, power, control, or a thousand differing combinations of these dividends. The problem comes when the payoff is not what we want or when it is not what the other person wants. Then the trouble begins.

Gary Inrig warns in his excellent book, *Quality Friendship,*

> Friendship is built upon mutual attraction, but there is a problem with attraction we must notice. We can be attracted to others because of a lack of love in our lives. We may see the other person primarily as someone who can meet our needs, and, as we shall see, such a negative basis can have devastating results.[3]

Healthy is always a worthy goal. You cannot, however, make anyone else healthy. That is something they have to pursue for themselves. You can model health, you can speak healthy words (the Bible calls that "wholesome"), and you can pray for your friend, but you cannot give her health. One of the subtle myths that mark relationships that are marred and too close to the fire is the responsibility one person bears for the emotional, spiritual, and/or physical health of the other person.

Early in my journey, a wise counselor told me something that has stuck with me for a long time. I was struggling with a relationship with someone I truly thought needed me in her life for myriad reasons, but primarily so I could help her heal emotionally!

It was too daunting, too much, too hard, and as I explained this to the counselor she said, "Jan, you cannot be another person's mother, pastor, or shrink!" Her words grabbed my mind. I had to push my behavior through that grid, and when I did, I saw that I had tried to be all of those—and although I was sincere, I had failed to bring about change. Instead, I found myself in an unhealthy relationship. I had not made the other person healthy. Instead, I had become unhealthy. The relationship was not immoral, but it was unhealthy. And as long as I was a part of it, I could see only that there was a need and I was failing to meet it. What I couldn't see was that I was attempting to do something God never intended me to do. I was trying to fulfill a role that God had not equipped me to fill.

Therefore, I was frustrated, angry, and hurt. That's no way to live! Those feelings are among the first clues that you have a problem. And since the truth is that you cannot make another's choices for him, you have to take responsibility to make your own choices. I made the only choice I could make. I left the relationship and asked God to heal both of us. I knew there was no way we would have a healthy relationship unless God opened our eyes, and since that had not happened to both of us, I knew it was better not to relate. The relationship had been founded on the wrong principles with the wrong goals, so it was necessary to end it in order not to perpetuate the same lack of health for a longer period of time.

You may be saying, "But, but, but . . . that doesn't sound loving." That is one of Satan's ploys. He loves to accuse us when we do the hard thing. It is so much easier to maintain a relational quagmire than to make choices that are healthy. You do all that you can to live at peace, according to the Scriptures, but ongoing sickness does nothing for you or the other person.

Healthy relationships are not always perfect. Two people who are trying to relate to one another will encounter differences, but friendship is the open acceptance of your friend for who she is. It is not the sick need to control her, change her, or make her responsible for your well-being. That is playing with a fire that will burn.

FIRE-PROOFING YOUR FRIENDSHIPS

In her booklet *Emotional Dependency,* Lori Thorkelson Rentzel lists some ways emotionally dependent people get entangled in relationships that are headed for deep trouble. Some of them are listed below.

- Finances: combining finances and personal possessions such as property and furniture and/or moving in together.
- Gifts: giving gifts and cards regularly for no special occasion [such as flowers, jewelry, baked goods, and gifts symbolic of the relationship]. . . .
- Needing "help": creating or exaggerating problems to gain attention and sympathy. . . .

- Pouting, brooding, cold silences: when asked, "What's wrong?" an emotionally dependent person might reply by sighing and saying, "Nothing."
- Time: keeping the other's time occupied so as not to allow for separate activities.[4]

If you are experiencing any of this in your relationship, you might want to back up and take another look at what's going on with you and your friend. Are you caught in a trap that is teetering on the edge of the Enemy's fire pit? Are you controlling or being controlled to the point where you cannot even recognize your own heart and your own heart's motive? Are your emotions too raw for you to hear what God has been telling you?

Then you are ready to stop and ask for a good truth bath. Take the time to sit and soak in God's Word. In the quiet, ask Him to silence the crowd in your mind and speak to your heart. Listen carefully and see what He says to you. He longs to communicate with us, but because of the crowd and the roar of our world, it can be hard to hear Him. The listening is up to you. As you quietly sit and ask Him to speak, you will hear Him, if ever so faintly. Just don't give up. He loves you and created you to be in intimate communion with Him.

It is usually relationships that cause us to dance around fire pits. Strangely enough, it is the Enemy's tactic to suggest that because God is holding out on us and because He doesn't mean what He says, we can do what we want to do and be what we want to be in our relationships. And somehow, we can find a salve for our souls.

Relationships are wonderful, but when they don't fit God's prescription for what is good for us, no matter what you do, you will find yourself playing with fire.

I watched a talk show where a woman who had once been very overweight said that all she had ever been was a wife and a mommy, but now that she had trimmed the fat off her body, she needed the mental stimulation of a male companion she enjoyed being with. She protested that there was nothing between her and her boyfriend but mental stimulation. Her husband, sitting next to her, said he was unable to accept it. She said, in essence, "Too bad." She needed the stimulation. Interestingly, the host of the show, who is a woman, loudly protested that there was nothing wrong with the woman's having a relationship with a man who was not her husband. Going to lunch and talking on the phone shouldn't be a problem, she protested.

The subtle suggestion of the Enemy is that, of course, there is nothing wrong with such "innocent" behavior. But the fruit it was producing was sour, and despite her many complaints to the contrary, it was obvious she wasn't growing. At this point, she was stuck in her stubborn determination to have it her way. She had yet to see what the results would be for her, for her marriage, and for the man with whom she needed stimulation.

We can convince ourselves of anything. But I have discovered that when the people around us express concern, it is probably a good idea to check our motives. There is a reason God puts people in our lives who are willing to tell us the truth even if we become offended.

The Scriptures say, "Faithful are the wounds of a friend, but deceitful are the kisses of an enemy" (Proverbs 27:6). Faithful, truth-speaking friends are a gift from God. Listening to them is one of the best ways to put up a fire wall between you and a relationship that takes you over the line.

DANGEROUS PEOPLE FIRE

People can be dangerous. They don't have to be close to you to cause damage. They just have to be able to get to you. This person can be a neighbor, an acquaintance at work, someone you know at your church, or anyone with whom you have to interact. Through fear, guilt, anger, and a host of other weapons, such persons leave you emotionally crippled whenever you encounter them. It seems that the hardest thing for a Christian to do is to avoid someone like that. This is not the beloved pagan who is just a little ornery at times, but this is the individual who seems to have an agenda for your life—to kill, steal, and destroy. He or she will stamp out your joy and stomp on your dreams through verbal put-downs and ongoing angry interactions. It is the kind of individual who breathes a fire of his own.

You can tangle with this person if you want to, but the result will always be the same. You will be hurt, destroyed, and devalued just a little bit more. Proverbs 13:20 says, "He who walks with wise men will be wise, but the companion of fools will suffer harm." You would not believe the excuses I hear for continuing to hang out with this kind of destructive person.

LeRoy Eims writes in *Be the Leader You Were Meant to Be*:

> Rattlesnakes are fairly common where I live. I encounter one almost every summer. It is a frightening experience to see a rattlesnake coiled, looking at you, ready to strike. He's lightning quick and accurate. I have a two-point program for handling rattlesnakes: shun and avoid. You don't need much insight to figure out what to do with something as dangerous as a diamondback rattler. You don't mess around.[5]

If you recognize a dangerous person in your life, then trust me, don't mess around! Shun and avoid! That is the way to keep yourself from being burned.

Don't go into denial or rationalization. If you are beat up and damaged every time you encounter this dangerous person, wouldn't wisdom say to you, "Shun and avoid"?

Silly women are not wise women. I don't know about you, but I would rather be wise, safe, and maybe even wrong than silly, burned, and wrong! Be careful; be aware. When you play close to a fire, you will be burned.

OTHER MATCHES

There are some other areas where playing with fire can quickly become deadly.

Lying

Lying is one of those. Avoiding the truth, changing the truth, denying the truth are ways to play with fire. When you believe God doesn't mean what He says and God is holding out on you, a little lie doesn't seem like such a big deal—but if God does mean what He says, then lying is big to Him. He was the one who said in a very clear-cut way, "You shall not bear false witness" (Exodus 20:16). You know when you are lying and you know how to stop it. It is only when you lie to yourself and rationalize it as partial truth that you can talk yourself into continuing to lie. Think about it. Is there some lie you are holding to and you are representing it as truth? Is there something you need to set straight because you just haven't wanted to face it? Now, please hear me on this. Not everyone needs to know everything about you. You are under no obligation to tell anything to anyone who has no need to know or who does not have a relationship with you that requires openness. But if you are keeping something hidden, it would be a good idea to ask the Lord to show you how you can tell it to the people in your life who need to know. Playing with a lie is playing with fire.

Recognizing and Avoiding the Liar

Another fiery problem is the how to recognize a liar and avoid him. Sometimes we women are slow to call a rat a rat even though we see his whiskers and the twitching of his nose. Being lied to and failing to recognize it is at the root of the whole myths problem. As small as a lie can seem to you, you can be part of either passing on the truth or passing on a lie. That's another reason to check yourself to see if you are believing a lie and possibly even passing it on. Too many of us have been seduced by the lies of those who do not have our best interest at heart. The Bible describes them as lovers of selves. Read the Word of the Lord:

> But realize this, that in the last days difficult times will come. For men will be lovers of self, lovers of money, boastful, arrogant, revilers, disobedient to parents, ungrateful, unholy, unloving, irreconcilable, malicious gossips, without self-control, brutal, haters of good, treacherous, reckless, conceited, lovers of pleasure rather than lovers of God, holding to a form of godliness, although they have denied its power; Avoid such men as these. For among them are those who enter into households and captivate weak women weighed down with sins, led on by various impulses, always learning and never able to come to the knowledge of the truth. (2 TIMOTHY 3:1–7)

God forbid that we who are women of God would find ourselves being weak because of our own sin. We are prime candidates for deception when we do not walk straight ourselves.

Sometimes you can be walking uprightly yourself but because you have been brainwashed, you succumb to something that you know is wrong. It has come from convincing sources, but still it is wrong.

Jeannette is a precious woman who has been caught in the backlash of a lie. She is married and is the mother of several children. I met her at the point in her life where she had been following her itinerate preacher husband around the country. They settled in several small communities, but frequently moved on. She was able to hold the family together until the children got older and began to struggle with the discipline their father meted out to them. Jeannette didn't like it, but she thought she had to allow it—at least that is what she had been told. Her husband called in the elders of the church to be part of the children's discipline. If they needed a paddling, the elders were called, and the children were lectured and paddled by these men. When I asked Jeannette why she let that go on, she said that it was the teaching of the church and she had never thought to question it until her son rebelled. She didn't like it, but her husband had convinced her that it was right. Needless to say, being lied to dangles you over a fire pit.

Satan loves it when we lie, and he loves to see to it that we are lied to. That's his nature.

Check out what Jesus Himself said about the Deceiver:

> *He was a murderer from the beginning, and does not stand in the truth because there is no truth in him. Whenever he speaks a lie, he speaks from his own nature, for he is a liar and the father of lies.* (JOHN 8:44)

When you deal in lies—telling them or hearing them—you engage the archliar of them all, Satan. He hates the truth, but you can know that when you speak the truth and look for the truth, you are evading his grasp on your mind and heart.

THE MYTH
OF LOVE

I have been a conference speaker for a lot of years, and it has always been interesting to me how we women respond to the subject of love. If you talk about traditional ways of loving, the tears will flow every time. We love to love! We love the romanticism of it, the sweetness of it, the gentle, unflappable tenderness of love. It taps into our motherly nature. We are nurturers, and we enjoy that part of the assignment.

We all want to love and be loved in a way that *feels* good.

Greeting card companies make millions from our desire to somehow express a love that is different from all others, a love that is deeply committed. All of us probably have a drawer where there is a little stack of sentimental cards with words of undying love swirled across the front of each delicate offering. Yet whether they are cards that we have given and saved after the object of our love has read them, or cards that we have received, let's face it, that drawer full cards is not what love is all about.

LOVE ISN'T ALWAYS PRETTY

The major myth about love and a love relationship is that it always looks pretty and feels good. We want the objects of our love to be pretty, act pretty, and make us feel good. That is just the raw bottom line. Because of that myth, too often we are faced with the fact that real love has nothing to do with "prettiness" or "good feelings." Real love has to do with commitment and choices. It is the overarching principle in a meaningful relationship.

If you are contemplating marriage, married, formerly married, or never married, understanding the truth about love in relationships is one of the most significant myths to examine in order to clean up and maintain healthy relationships.

If you say you love someone and you mean that you love them in the purest sense possible, it means that you are committed to their highest good. That might be something different at any given moment, but the ultimate goal is their good, not some personal need of yours. That doesn't mean that you don't have needs. We all do. Rather, it is saying that you are not looking to another person to give you what he cannot or will not give, but that you are willing to extend something to him that he cannot earn or create for himself. *That* is when true love takes place. That is when you blow away the myths and get to the truth.

THIS IS WHAT LOVE LOOKS LIKE

In *Love Life for Every Couple,* Dr. Ed Wheat gives a clear description of this unconditional, "doesn't matter whether the other person cooperates or not" kind of love. In the Scriptures, it is referred to as *agape* love. It is a love that can come only from God, and it has His mark all over it. Humanly, it is not possible. Our flesh eradicates it, but God gives us a way to come up with that love from our wills—not from our feelings. Wheat writes:

> "God's love has been poured out in our hearts through the Holy Spirit Who has been given to us" (Romans 5:5 AMPLIFIED). This is the *agape* love of the New Testament—unconditional, unchanging, inexhaustible, generous, beyond measure, and most wonderfully kind! . . .

We can make these observations concerning agape:

(1) *Agape* love means action, not just a benign attitude.

(2) *Agape* love means involvement, not a comfortable detachment from the needs of others.

(3) *Agape* loves means unconditionally loving the unlovable, the underserving, and the unresponsive.

(4) *Agape* love means permanent commitment to the object of one's love.

(5) *Agape* love means constructive, purposeful giving based not on blind sentimentality but on knowledge, the knowledge of what is best for the beloved.

(6) *Agape* love means consistency of behavior showing an ever-present concern for the beloved's highest good.

(7) *Agape* love is the chief means and the best way of blessing your partner and your marriage.[1]

When you see a list like that, do you think, "Whoa, that is huge. I don't think I can do that or even want to love like that because first of all, I have needs, and secondly, I am exhausted trying to love my difficult beloved person."

Well, I believe the myth we get tangled in so easily is that love means you are sentimental, mushy, powerless, and without options. That seems to be the message most women have gotten. Consequently, some of us have abdicated to that concept and have found ourselves living in unrealistic and stunting arrangements. Others of us have said, "If that is what love is, I can't do it! I can't live a sentimental, powerless life, pretending to love someone who is difficult and emotionally dangerous." What we have missed, my sisters, is that love is neither of these. It is a desire for the other person's highest good. It isn't a weak abdication to be sucked into the other person's craziness.

Two factors are at work here. We are living in emotionally hard days. Certain behaviors have increased that a few years ago happened far less frequently. A few years ago, if a man had a girly magazine tucked away in the garage, it rarely was a reason for more than a major annoyance in a marriage relationship.

If a kid slipped behind the house to smoke, it wasn't mind altering.

If a grandmother went off the deep end, it was usually a hormonal imbalance that eventually evened itself out. It wasn't a torrid affair with someone she met on the Internet.

If a pastor got himself into trouble, it was because he had offended the man with the biggest stack of money in the church. It wasn't because he embezzled church funds and planned to leave town with his secretary.

If a youth leader was out of touch it wasn't nearly as devastating as the youth leader touching kids where they should never be touched.

These things went on for sure, but they have proliferated to a point that you probably won't be able to avoid having your love tested by some sort of irrational assault from truly irrational behavior.

The Bible is clear that in the last days, things are going to be different. Read the Word of the Lord from 2 Timothy 3:1–9:

> *But realize this, that in the last days difficult times will come. For men will be lovers of self, lovers of money, boastful, arrogant, revilers, disobedient to parents, ungrateful, unholy, unloving, irreconcilable, malicious gossips, without self-control, brutal, haters of good, treacherous, reckless, conceited, lovers of pleasure rather than lovers of God, holding to a form of godliness, although they have denied its power; Avoid such men as these. For among them are those who enter into households and captivate weak women weighed down with sins, led on by various impulses, always learning and never able to come to the knowledge of the truth. Just as Jannes and Jambres opposed Moses, so these men also oppose the truth, men of depraved mind, rejected in regard to the faith. But they will not make further progress; for their folly will be obvious to all.*

If the behavior of so many we hear about is any indication, we are getting closer and closer to the end. In light of that, the question begs to be asked: How can we women love with an agape love and be right before God? How can we understand what real love is and escape being destroyed?

WHAT IS REAL LOVE?

I truly believe that we have to cut through the myth of sentimentality and get down to the hard work of doing what is right for the other person. Satan hates that because when you wake up and realize that is what is required of you, the chains of obligation and the mushy haze of pseudolove begin to fall away. You enter into a hard, tough walk of faith in the face of great emotional struggle. But what we often forget is that we have the power of the Holy Spirit within us if we are born again. That power is *dunamis;* it is dynamite; and we can do whatever it takes when we realize that it is right and that it is God who is empowering us to do the hard thing.

Here is what doing the hard thing can look like:

- A precious woman married to a physician spoke with pleading in her voice, "We are getting ready to move again." (Her husband had been in his current practice just two years as long as he usually managed to stick with any postion.) She said, "He is cheating on our income tax, messing up our finances to the point where we have no savings, and is involved in pornography. What do I do? We have four small children, and I am without any skills for supporting us."

  What would be the agape love thing to do?

- Hattie is caring for her mother, who lives in her home. The mother is not ill; she is, however, what most people would call mean. She is widowed, but she is only in her sixties and could work. However, she refuses, and she tells Hattie on a regular basis that she is just giving back what she owes. The mother listens in on phone conversations and if anyone comes by the house, she parks herself in the middle of the conversation, contributing her own form of acidic comment.

  What would be the agape love thing to do?

- Georgette's daughter decided to get pregnant so that she could have another baby to love. Georgette is torn in pieces. She already cares for her daughter's two other children by her first and second husbands. They are four- and three-years-old. When her daughter announced that she was now pregnant by her boyfriend, Georgette's heart sank in despair. She knows that her daughter will not care for this child any better than she cares for the other two. Georgette's dilemma is not what to do with her daughter. She is strong in her resolve to let her face the consequences of her sin. Her problem is what to do with the children.

How can she be a loving grandmother who has their best interest at heart?

- Maxine is married to a second husband, who is emotionally abusive. He also has become very ill and needs a liver transplant. They had been married for just a few months when she realized she was living the life of an abused woman and learned about her husband's illness. Her children are in disbelief. How could she involve herself with this man? How could she spend her finishing years taking care of someone who might just finish her?

What is agape love in this situation?

I think you can see that it isn't always as simple as it looks. How would you describe agape love to any or all of these people? The answer is, you couldn't. Agape love looks different in every situation. The myth is to believe that we can apply the same love application in every case. The key to discerning true agape love is to ask the Source of all true love, even though it is hard to know what to do. If you just assume you know what to do, you won't recognize if you are operating out of mythical thinking or are operating out of truth. The only source you have for loving in the way that is right and healthy is God Himself. He knows the need, He knows the future, He knows what will benefit the one who is loved, and He knows what will keep you in balance. See what God says in James 1:2–8:

> *Consider it all joy, my brethren, when you encounter various trials, knowing that the testing of your faith produces endurance. And let endurance have its perfect result, so that you may be perfect and complete, lacking in nothing.*
>
> *But if any of you lacks wisdom, let him ask of God, who gives to all generously and without reproach, and it will be given to him. But he must ask in faith without any doubting, for the one who doubts is like the surf of the sea, driven and tossed by the wind. For that man ought not to expect that he will receive anything from the Lord, being a double-minded man, unstable in all his ways.*

What is clear is this: When you don't know what to do, ask God.

> *But if any of you lacks wisdom, let him ask of God, who gives to all generously and without reproach, and it will be given to him.* (JAMES 1:5)

If you ask six people, you will get six opinions of what love would look like in your situation, and you still won't know what the best thing to do might be. People give us their opinion out of their own grid, background, personal bias, and religious experience.

I heard a tape about loving a husband, and the premise was, "Whatever he wants, go along with it!" The speaker called that submission. Her illustrations were from her own experience. She believed that the only way a wife could biblically relate to a man was to make him king and follow his every decree. Mutuality was nowhere mentioned. It was a one-sided, childlike obedience to one who occupied the male throne.

That may sound good and sacrificial if you look at it on the surface, but there was nothing whole or healthy about it. It certainly was not doing what was best for the husband. If we are going to be a helper "fit for him," our contributions need to be significant. For love to be meaningful, it has to risk questioning. No one does well who is given the power to be a dictator for life. That isn't what is best for him. Ultimately, it will cripple him. True agape love does not cripple.

Equally clear is the mandate to trust God when He tells you what to do.

> *But he must ask in faith without any doubting, for the one who doubts is like the surf of the sea, driven and tossed by the wind.* (JAMES 1:6)

There are times that it seems as if what God tells you to do is not right—at least it doesn't feel right, so we spend a lot of time trying to figure out how to alter His plan. God warns that the worst thing you can do is ask and then act as if He has given you the wrong answer.

> *But he must ask in faith without any doubting, for the one who doubts is like the surf of the sea, driven and tossed by the wind. For that man ought*

not to expect that he will receive anything from the Lord, being a double-minded man, unstable in all his ways. (JAMES 1:6–8)

Therein is the issue. So often we are unstable in our love because we have bought into the myth that love is always a sentimental, weak, sugarcoated response to someone's need. I like what Paul told the Thessalonian believers:

> *Live in peace with one another. We urge you, brethren, admonish the unruly, encourage the fainthearted, help the weak, be patient with everyone. See that no one repays another with evil for evil, but always seek after that which is good for one another and for all people.* (1 THESSALONIANS 5:13B–15)

I like the way Eugene Peterson paraphrased this Scripture in *The Message:*

> Get along among yourselves, each of you doing your part. Our counsel is that you warn the freeloaders to get a move on. Gently encourage the stragglers, and reach out for the exhausted, pulling them to their feet. Be patient with each person, attentive to individual needs. And be careful that when you get on each other's nerves you don't snap at each other. Look for the best in each other, and always do your best to bring it out![2]

GROWING UP AND DOING HARD THINGS

Given that wise and timely admonition, let's talk about the hard job of being grown up and doing hard things. Doing what is best for the other person is often hard because it doesn't always look best. And for our loved one, it often does not feel best, either. But if God has told you in response to your question that you should move in a certain way, He expects you to do that.

I talked with a dear woman who thought it was totally ungodly to rein in her husband from his adulterous affairs. She tried to make a statement to him by leaving him for four days, but she couldn't stand to think about him doing his own laundry, so she came home.

He relaxed when she came home and went back to his lover. His wife was devastated. She claimed to love him but also claimed to be unable to leave him. Love doesn't act like that in the face of betrayal. True agape love does what is best for the other person. It allows the consequences to bring repentance. To just go along with her husband's philandering was not best for him, nor did it create any love and respect between them. He knew he could do whatever he wanted to and walk all over his wife. That was not love. She knew that he was going to do whatever he wanted to and then give lip service to his love for her. She couldn't face the fact that if they were ever going to have a healthy marriage, her love needed to be strong, hard-nosed, and respectful of him as well as of her own well-being. The last I heard from them, both were still looking pitiful, acting the way they always had acted—and the pain was excruciating. Love looked as if it had failed, but it hadn't, really, because it wasn't truly love.

CHOOSING TO LOVE

It is hard to come to the point where you recognize you have no feelings. It isn't that you have bad feelings toward the one you loved, but that you have *no* feelings. Whatever has happened between you has dumped a huge bucket of cold water on a delicate little flame, and there is not even a spark left.

If you feel that way, it may be that you have said to people around you, "I have fallen out of love!" Or maybe someone has come to you and said, "I never did love you." Whether you are the one who has gone numb or you are the one who has been told that there are no feelings left, you are crushed. You never meant for it to be this way. Even during the time that some painful things were going on, you could always at least drag up a little anger, a little agitation. Now, though, you feel nothing or you know that the other person feels nothing for you.

But neither of these situations means that there is no love between you. The myth that entangles our understanding of love is the idea that you have to have a feeling with love. The other part of that myth is that those feelings must be sweet and full of sentimental appreciation for the original object of your affection. Believing that myth leaves you convinced you have fallen out of love, and that there is no hope for you since you don't feel anything.

You may feel like the woman who wrote this poem.

–IN THOSE DAYS–

the words, "I love you, honey,"
were said with five different inflections
and meant fifty different things.
They could have meant
thank you for opening the catsup bottle,
even though you said that I had loosened it first,
Or I enjoy our talks
when you come home from work
and there's just the two of us to share and dream.
Or simply that I appreciate all those things
that make up you:
your sensitive strength
the way you smile me off my soapbox,
or the way you pretend you are listening
when you read the paper.
But somewhere along the way we turned
and instead of floating with the current,
we now struggle against it.
It wasn't one action, or one word,
but a series of little unresolved spats and quarrels
that now make the TV the solution
to the problems of a hard day
and silences us when we should say
"Thank you" or "You really look nice today."
Today, I no longer tell you that I love you
because the sound of those words
mocks the special meaning that they carried
when we were first wed,
and it is too painful to remember
that those feelings we said we would never lose
were, tear by tear, left in the past.

—DEBORAH JEAN MORRIS SWINDOLL, March 2, 1980

This experience of "no feelings" may not even be taking place in a marital relationship. You may have a friend who was once dear to your heart, but time and too many disagreements and hurts have intervened and you feel nothing for her any longer. Maybe it is a sister, or a mother, or—yes, it happens—maybe it's your child.

If you choose to forgive (send away the offense, if you can remember what it is) and seek to think of one good thing about the other person, you will begin to feel. It may not be much, but it will be a gentle wind that blows the flame to life. One of the best things you can do is set your internal tape player on Philippians 4:8–9

> *Finally, brethren, whatever is true, whatever is honorable, whatever is right, whatever is pure, whatever is lovely, whatever is of good repute, if there is any excellence and if anything worthy of praise, dwell on these things. . . . and the God of peace will be with you.*

As you do this, ask God to restore some feeling. Ask Him to give you what you need to love the way He wants you to love. He may give you a love that is tender and moldable to the other person. He may give you a love that is firm and just, but a love nonetheless. God will give you what you need to love the way He wants you to for any given situation. You just have to be willing to hear His voice and trust that He is speaking. The main thing to factor in is that "love never fails" (1 Corinthians 13:8). Whether it is tough or tender, ultimately love has to respond to the object that once captured it.

And the only way you can love in God's way is to surrender to what He wants to do in you. You cannot drum up love or make yourself "feel," but you can let God love through you as you surrender to Him. Why not make this poem your prayer as we leave this chapter?

– TAKE OVER –

At first, Lord, I asked You
To take sides with me.
With David the Psalmist
I circled and underlined:
"The Lord is for me . . ."

"Maintain my rights, O Lord . . ."
"Let me stand before my foes . . ."
But with all my pleading
I lay drenched in darkness
Until in utter confusion I cried
"Don't take sides, Lord,
Just take over."
And suddenly it was morning.

—RUTH HARMS CALKIN, *TELL ME AGAIN, LORD, I FORGET*

CHAPTER ELEVEN

THE MYTH OF CHURCH IS ALWAYS A SAFE PLACE

Before we even begin this chapter discussion, I think it would be good to make a disclaimer. I love the body of Christ, the church. I love the people of God, and I believe that apart from the presence of the church on this earth, God would have shut the whole thing down a long time ago. So when I write about "church myths," it is not with a spirit of despair or disgust. Rather, it is with the desire to say, one church member to another, "Look at us. What are we doing here?"

We who make up the church are a motley bunch, desperately in need of one another. We are aliens in a foreign land where we are misunderstood and maligned. That's a fact. But sometimes we fail to see that we bring a lot of our grief on ourselves by our plastic, pigheaded ways. We hold to the truth, but so often we fail to look at what is happening in the lives of people in the body who are having that truth applied to them. For so many people who have asked for our help to be lying wounded and bleeding around our periphery, there have to be myths buzzing around the truth we hold.

There is a myth in the land that "church is a safe place." For many women, the rude awakening is that not *every* church is a safe place. Some churches are very safe and the women who attend them are nourished, growing believers, but many churches are houses of frustration. I would like to think that this happens where there is misunderstanding rather than misbehavior. I still have the optimism to believe that if good people see that their understanding of the truth is causing damage, they will work to understand and stop it.

It would also be good for those who misbehave to stop what they are doing, but I have little hope that just bringing their misdeeds to their attention will stop them. I truly hope that most of the agony comes from good people who just don't understand. They have bought into a tradition that includes mythical components, and it has never occurred to them that what they are doing is not working. Perhaps they have been deceived by myths saturated with traditions, wrong attitudes, and cultural bias.

FEELINGS OF MISUNDERSTANDING

As I travel, I encounter women who feel misunderstood by their church leadership. I have run across it so often, I can confidently say that this is neither a local nor a regional problem. It is a common complaint wherever women's distinctive needs are not taken into consideration. I often think that misunderstandings about women are tangled with the man-woman myths that float through the air. Commenting on the way things are in her world, one sharp woman summed it up this way: "It's the husband's job to fix the wife. It's the wife's job to fix what's wrong in the marriage. Either way, it's her problem." That is the way it appears to many women who have turned to the church for help.

———————————— ✥ ————————————

RING AROUND THE COLLAR

"Wives feel resentment when it is assumed that they are responsible for everything that goes wrong around the house. This is epitomized in the television ad in which the husband is upset because there's a 'ring around the collar.' The wife breaks into tears because her detergent has not removed the dirt from her husband's shirt. The ring around the collar is seen as telltale evidence of her failure.

"*The ad never asks the obvious question: 'Why didn't he wash his neck?'*"

—*Tony Campolo*

———————————— ✥ ————————————

Granted, that isn't always the case. Some women refuse to take responsibility for any problem and manage to become the greater part of their fiascoes, but generally speaking, this bright woman's comments are true.

The nurturing part of women sets us up to carry the brunt of the responsibility for fixing problems. Of course, since it is the woman who is the one usually willing to seek help for marital distress, it is understandable that church leadership might think we are the logical ones to handle what must be done. What hurts my heart is that many women who seek help and believe they will find it are devastated when they realize that they have been made the ones responsible for the problems.

More than one woman who has gone for help at her church has met overwhelming cynicism. So often it is insinuated that things are not as bad as she says or that she has created the problem by her behavior. Women I have encountered typically have encountered a lot of law. Sometimes someone in leadership extends grace, but more often than not there is standoffishness. Maybe this occurs because it is hard for godly men to believe that other men could actually behave in the atrocious ways the women are describing. They would never treat their wives that way, so just deny the report. It is much easier to pretend it wasn't that bad.

The errors seem to fall into the categories of denial or control. A woman we will call Laura went to her pastor when she had been completely stripped of all hope for her marriage. Her husband, George, was involved in multiple affairs. Her pastor totally supported her as long as she just went along, trying to hold things together while George went in and out of their marriage. When she finally filed for divorce, any ongoing support from her pastor immediately ceased. Despite the fact she had biblical grounds for ending the marriage, she didn't have actual physical proof of her husband's affairs. Her word wasn't good enough, and because she was unable to present the kind of proof her pastor would believe, he abandoned her. Not only did he abandon her, but the people in the church abandoned her as well. She became persona non grata.

Finally, turning from the place and the people who should have stood with her, Laura herself had an affair, and she was caught. She was wrong. No way around it. But I have to wonder what happened to love and compassion when the pastor cast her out of the church and her church friends turned their backs on her. She had sinned and admitted it, but still she was banished from the church.

The obvious choice at this point was to go where she thought she was loved. Left with no support at all, she finally married the man with whom she had the affair. Her first husband was never chastised for his behavior. But she was caught, and that settled the problem for the church. Obviously, they had discovered what was wrong all along. It was Laura. The rules and regulations were far more important than compassionate reconciliation.

Then there was Sara Beth, who would have divorced her abusive husband years ago but chose to stay with him for thirty-five violence-filled years. She stayed with him for one reason. Her church told her that if she divorced her husband that would sever her from them. Not only would they bar her from continuing to serve as a Sunday school teacher, but they would not even allow her to attend classes. Interesting dilemma. No win, no win!

Then there was Angela, who led the children's choir at her church. She discovered her husband's deep involvement with pornography, and after many anguished encounters, asked him to leave their home until he could get his life-controlling sin under management. Although they had gone to their pastor for counseling, and it was clear that her husband was wrong and unrepentant, she was asked to give up any involvement in her church activities because *she* asked *him* to leave. Her husband left the scene, and she was left behind to receive correction from the leadership.

CHURCH MYTHS

At the most vulnerable time in their lives, these women and myriad others have had to face the fact that they were alone. If they sought help and took responsibility for their own well-being and that of their family, they were faced with demeaning encounters with church leadership they had loved. My question is, "Where is it written?" Why does the woman bear the brunt for the misbehavior of her husband? I realize that many a man has borne the brunt of a wife's indiscretion, but from what I have observed, women are the greatest burden bearers when it comes to making the home situation work. This comes from one of the myths perpetuated by the church, that the *woman* sets the atmosphere in the home. Does she? Or could it be that she can do her part to make the atmosphere as pleasant as possible, but it requires the cooperation of everyone under the roof to establish a positive atmosphere.

For years there has been teaching that has put the mother lode of responsibility on the woman. The following are some notes from a lesson taught several years ago by a long-forgotten speaker. (Since I am a speaker, I know it doesn't take several years to forget us, but this one truly was years ago and the speaker truly is forgotten.) These thoughts seem biblical on the surface. But look closer and process them through the eyes of a woman trying to walk a godly walk while married to an ungodly man. Is she to check her brains at the door and live like this? Think it through and ask yourself, "Where is it written?"

The greatest way to please God is to please your husband.

This idea sounds good, but what if the husband can't be pleased? A woman could become a total wreck, always striving to please someone who won't be pleased. Allowing the Holy Spirit to live through her while displaying the fruit of love, joy, peace, patience, kindness, and self-control is another story. Pleasing a man who can't be pleased and allowing the life of Christ to be lived through your body are two different things. Yet because we don't ask the question, "Where is it written?" it is easy to become candidates for bondage and failure.

Do what the husband wants before he wants it. You should have such an attitude of servanthood that you know what will make your husband successful and do it even before he realizes his goals.

Think that one through. The focus is on the man, not on Christ. If you are serving Christ, you will honor your husband by loving him in the way that seeks his good. He may be such a poor planner that if you do for him before he wants it, he will forever depend on you to think for him. That sounds like a mother role to me—finish your son's term paper before he asks and that will make him successful. Pick up after your husband and that will make him great. What kind of mythical thinking is that?

When a wife is willing to suffer, she can heal her husband.

What about a woman who is being abused? What does her suffering do for her husband other than give him more guilt, shame, anger, and power? I really have to ask, "Where is it written?" on this one.

Only totally innocent suffering, not rebellion, is God's will.

I understand the point of this. Don't bring suffering on yourself with a rebellious spirit. But if you encounter powerful, godless behavior, there is a point to rebelling—and if you suffer, you suffer.

God will use a husband in the wife's life as a chisel to make her more like Jesus. If you run, God is going to raise up another instrument. The husband is an extension of God's hand.

The myths that waft through this statement make me dizzy. Where is it written that a husband or a wife is a chisel? God uses circumstances and trials to do the work of maturing, but this statement makes the person the instrument. And that is all it takes for some people to become power happy. Being a chisel is a picture of authority and control they would just love to assume.

Even God is painted as power happy. He is going to get you one way or the other, so you might as well submit to the chisel that is chipping away at you. Since the husband is an *extension* of God's *hand,* the wife becomes the one under that hand to be chipped away at. That picture comes from the chisel metaphor. It may be that the husband is an extension of God's love and care, but that is not the picture that is painted. This whole metaphor makes God look angry and determined to *chisel, chip, crack,* and *break.* I understand the deep mercy of the Lord, but to tangle that with a husband who is controlling and angry gives a warped view of God, husbands, wives, and life. God disciplines those He loves, but that discipline is for correction, guidance, and growth, not for breaking, chipping, and cracking.

I have noticed that anytime there is a relational truth between men and women that takes on mythical qualities, it has to do with power. The stronger gets the rewards while the weaker is pushed down. How like Satan to swish his obnoxious tail through the precious truth of God's Word and leave people in confusion about God and each other. Interestingly, in some churches male dominance and power is fed by a mythical understanding of God and His ways, and in other churches female dominance and power is fed by a mythical understanding of God and His ways. Either extreme makes the church an unsafe place for women.

Knowing God and knowing His ways through His Word is the *only* way to be safe. Extremes that create divisiveness miss the qualities of peace, unity, and love that are the mark of God.

WOMEN, LEADERSHIP, QUESTIONS

Many men in church leadership earnestly believe the myth that we women need someone to protect us from ourselves. We need the men as the guardians of our souls. Now, it's true that if we have good leaders who want the best for us and are willing to wade through the deep waters with us, we would be fools to shun that. Church would then be a safe place, a place where correction and encouragement would be intertwined with love.

It is another story when women are viewed as children and are put in the position to be taken care of as children. Church then becomes a dangerous place for women. It all goes sour when an adult woman is seen as anything less than a fully functioning adult in need of and deserving the same respect as any man.

My view on this has nothing to do with making God into a woman and men into less than men. Those are perversions that obliterate the truth. It has to do with allowing women to be the women God the Father made them to be. It is about allowing women the privilege of using their gifts and impacting the body for good. God has not handed out the spiritual gifts with a gender bias. Giftedness is just that—giftedness. The order God has set up for the structure of the church is His as well. There are certain offices that are reserved for males—that is not a problem. But it is a problem when a female has the character, the gifts, and the leadership to do a mighty work for God and is not allowed to do so for one reason: she is female.

The following thoughts, written by a godly young woman, sum it up well:

> If you want to know what it's like to be a woman leader in the church, just listen. Not to what women say. Listen instead to what women hear. Try to hear specifically what the rest of the Christian community is telling them.
>
> Once you do, I think you will find that people in the church reliably send mixed messages to women leaders that at once say yes and no. We say "yes" to them as women, and "no" to them as leaders. If a woman hears the "yes," then she'll feel affirmed, and not understand why another woman sees a problem. But if she hears the "no," she'll feel disrespected and hurt.
>
> The dynamic goes like this. As long as a woman leader is perceived primarily to be a Christian woman, all is well. But the moment she emerges as a Christian leader, things begin to change. Christian women are wise, insightful, and gentle. But we're not so sure about Christian women who lead. Thus a Christian woman leader must ever prove herself to be more woman than leader for as long as she continues to lead.

To be a woman leader is to hear a contradictory message from the church. On the one hand, women leaders are told they can do all things through Christ (Philippians 4:13). They can step out into the mission field and evangelize a whole nation. They can disciple a king, rebuke a false teacher, correct a wayward brother, and change the course of history by their prayers. They can lead or preach to thousands as long as the appropriate men invite them to. And if their leadership is more suited for work outside the church, then they can become senators, or CEOs, or even President. There's really nothing they can't do.

Though many Christian women would rather not admit it, Christian women leaders are caught between two undesirable choices: (1) They can retreat from the center of action, bow their heads, and flee willingly to the refuge of "femininity"; (2) they can plunge into the center of action, shake their fists, and fight for women's rights to total equality.

The most important thing for Christian men to understand is that Christian women don't want to flee or fight. We simply want to go forward. We want to be like Esther, who went forward to make a request of the king, even though her presence was unsolicited and unlawful (Esther 4:11). Esther neither fought nor fled. Instead, she went forward and broke the social norms of her culture. Esther went forward because God called her to go forward. So heartfelt were her convictions that she resolved to risk her very life. "If I perish, I perish," she said (Esther 4:16).[1]

It is important for *everyone* to be able to exercise his or her gifts and calling appropriately.

Is it not possible to lead without offending our brothers? Is it not possible to support them in what they do while they support us in what we do? Would that not be the more Christlike model to follow?

I saw this very thing demonstrated in a beautiful way while I was speaking at a church several years ago. This whole body could not do enough to express their loving concern. From the moment I arrived, I found little surprises that said, "You are special." I felt loved and cared for, but I had no idea how the initial acts of this loving welcome would only deepen throughout the weekend.

On Saturday morning as I prepared to speak, the director of the retreat quietly said, "Jan, would you mind if we go have prayer with the men?" Other than the sound tech, I hadn't seen a man anywhere, but

I agreed.

I was taken aback when we stepped into a small, dark room right next to the platform area where I would speak in a few minutes. Five men were waiting. They invited me to sit down, and then they began to pray tender prayers of loving support, affirmation, and blessing. They prayed Scripture back to the Lord on my behalf, asking Him to work in us all that He wanted to work that day. When they concluded, they said, "We'll be in this room all day, praying for you. If you have a need, just let us know. We will be here."

Needless to say, as I led the conference that day, the thought that there were five men in the next room interceding for the women and for me brought me incredible comfort, confidence, and—more than anything—a sense of respect. I felt safe. These men cared what happened to the women who were in their church for that day. Not only were they praying, but each one prepared a letter that was read to the women at the beginning of every session. They were letters filled with scriptural exhortation and tender care. They spoke words that said, "We care about you because we are your brothers in Christ."

In the company of these men, there was a sense of value. I was free to exercise my gifts, and they cheered me on. I cheered them as they went about what God had called them to do. It was a time of mutual respect for who we all were in Christ. I didn't resent their position, nor did they resent or fear mine. We all knew what Andrew Murray meant when he wrote, "I am here by 'God's Appointment, Under His Keeping, For His Time.'" In this knowledge, we all, men and women alike, found joy in Christ and in one another. That kind of environment breeds safety for women as well as for everyone else.

CHURCH SHOULD BE A SAFE PLACE FOR EVERYONE

The church will become a safe place for women only when it is a safe place for everyone—when people are viewed as precious no matter their gender, background, or race. It cannot be a place where one gender, one race, and one background has all of the power and no one else is allowed to participate fully. Love is the equalizing factor, but not everyone operates out of a heart that is overwhelmed with love toward people who are different.

The following story, which is all too true, displays the picture in a way that is impossible to miss. A wonderful social worker friend relates an incident where the background of people made a difference in the way they were treated by the church. It fits our premise. See what God shows you about yourself, both in the way that you are treated and the way that you treat other people.

> Years ago I led a Parents Anonymous Group for about five years. Most of the members were ex-convicts who were also child abusers. They were also very poor people. One of the local fitness centers allowed us to use their conference room for meetings and we found some teenagers who babysat with the children across the street at the local evangelical, Bible-believing church. This plan worked really well for a couple of years.
>
> One day the Education Director announced that the church was having a "shower" for the nursery and pre-school departments because there was a need for more toys. The next day, I got a call informing me that the *new* toys would be kept under lock and key in the cabinets and the Parents Anonymous children were not to play with them because they were too rough. (Now, these were poor kids who had *few* toys of their own.) I was told they *would*, however, be allowed to play with the *old, broken ones.* Well, as you can imagine, smoke came out my ears. I managed to get that one turned around, but it just broke my heart again to see that abused, broken children could not play with the best toys in Jesus' house—instead they were offered the broken trash!

You may be thinking, "But if they were rough and the toys were being broken that solution is not unreasonable." No, not if you want to preserve toys. It is not unreasonable. But, if children are a high priority, then shouldn't they be considered over a few new toys?

Think about it. The law over people. Toys over children and you can see where I am going. Toys and rowdy children weren't the issue in the next story. It was all about color—skin color—and it is the very worst church story I've heard.

It is told by a woman who lived it firsthand.

> We lived in a small town and were members of The First Church. There was an orphanage there, and the children attended our church.

In order to have added funding, the orphanage began to accept some federal funds. However, that meant that they took in black children for the first time. All of a sudden, when those "darling orphans" got off their bus in front of the church, there were several black children of all ages. They weren't called those "darling orphans" any longer!

My husband, Rick, taught the ten-year-olds' Sunday school class and a black young man, I'll call Charles, was in his class. Rick led him to Christ. That Sunday our pastor said something like, "Jesus loves you no matter who you are . . . where you come from . . . rich or poor . . ."; on and on. When we all stood to sing "Just as I Am," Charles walked to the front to confess his faith. Our pastor prayed with him, stalled, and awkwardly said, "Our church has a race policy. Before we welcome you into the church, we will have to have a church meeting." Charles was sent back to his seat.

You cannot imagine the furor that rose from that issue. It was absolutely vicious. One of the main comments of the older members was, "This is *our church* . . . *we* paid for it . . . it belongs to us and we don't want them here!"

Finally, the night came for the meeting. At the appropriate time, Rick rose and moved that we accept members regardless of race. A wave of anger and outrage swept through the church. They voted and we lost by one vote and from then on, those little *abused, orphaned* black children were brought to a church where they could not become members. They were rejected by the Body of Christ. They had *no home* anywhere and certainly *not* in the House of the Lord.

I know God must hang His head in grief when His earthly church acts so outrageously toward people He loves and for whom He died. I wish it weren't this way. I wish I could write a whole chapter about how safe and wonderful the church is for anyone who wants to be a part of it, and yet I know and you know that isn't true in every place. There are wonderful fellowships where servant leadership is practiced and no one is excluded from full participation in body life because of gender, race, or origin. May their tribe increase!

According to George Barna, who has his hand on the heartbeat of our Christian culture,

The big story is that people are people. They want substance from their church; they want to make a difference in the world through their church; and they need to feel connected to God and to other God-loving people as a result of their church experience. If those factors are in place, people will put up with a lot just so they can have these primary spiritual needs met. If a church does not satisfy these particular needs, people will feel spiritually unfulfilled and restless and probably search elsewhere for a church home.[2]

Wisdom dictates that you chose your church carefully.

A century ago the church that most Americans attended was virtually arranged for them at birth. Most people went to the church of their parents, which was the same church their grandparents had attended. Church shopping was an unknown practice. You changed churches when you moved, when the church went through a split, or when you entered a "mixed marriage"—meaning people from two different churches married and had to choose one or the other to attend.

Things have changed. Although Americans do not change churches as regularly as they change the brand of gasoline they use, church loyalty is a modern casualty. [3]

I would think that what is more important than any church loyalty is the quality of relationship that is possible. A healthy relationship based on mutual respect for one another, a high regard for the Scriptures, and a lavish devotion to Christ will make any church a safe place to attend. Problems will be there—that is part of our humanity. But respect, the Word, and the deep love of Jesus will keep problems in perspective and people protected no matter their gender, race, or background.

—————————————— ⁜ ——————————————

An article on the Barna Research Group, Ltd., Web site (http://www.barna.org), "Women Are the Backbone of the Christian Congregations in America" (6 March 2000), gives this report on the role of women in the church:

George Barna, president of the firm that conducted the research [on women in Christian congregations in America], commented about the role of men in the spiritual life of the family. In recent years, there has been a lot of talk about men and women sharing household responsibilities more equally. Despite such an egalitarian vision, in most cases, roles are still often determined based upon gender—but that is especially true when it comes to the responsibility for the family's spiritual health and growth. Women, more often than not, take the lead role in the spiritual life of the family. Women typically emerge as the primary—or only—spiritual mentor and role model for family members. And that puts a tremendous burden on wives and mothers.

If the Church is to stem the tide of biblical illiteracy and waning commitment to the Christian faith, men will have to reestablish themselves as partners and leaders of the spiritual functions of families. The family unit is the key for spiritual growth and maturation in our decentralized, relationally isolated culture. The apparent lack of spiritual leadership exhibited by millions of Christian men has significantly hampered the spiritual growth of tens of thousands of well-meaning but spiritually inert families. . . .

While Barna was upbeat about women's emphasis on faith, he sounded a note of caution regarding the high price women may pay for carrying excessive levels of spiritual responsibility. "While women represent the lion's share of Christians and the majority of participants in religious activities, many women appear to be burning out from their intense levels of involvement. Maybe most telling has been a 22% slip in church attendance since 1991 (55% to 45%). There has also been a 21% decline in the percentage of women who volunteer to help a church (29% in 1991 and 24% in 2000). Women's monumental effort to support the work of the Christian Church may be running on fumes."

Churches need to consider whether or not they are providing sufficient opportunities for women to receive ministry and not just provide ministry to others. We may continue to see tens of thousands of women leaving the church unless there is a widespread, aggressive, thoughtful approach to recognizing and appreciating women. At the same time we must impress upon men the importance that they model spiritual maturity and more actively participate in the life of the Church.

Barna also noted that another significant concern is the low levels of religious participation among women who are members of the Buster generation—those who are 34 and younger. For virtually every religious activity measured, Buster women— not unlike Buster men—were less likely than older generations to participate in such spiritual pursuits. The exception was meeting with a spiritual mentor or coach. Barna indicated that thus far it appears that the Church has not adequately addressed the needs of this generation.

───────────── ✛ ─────────────

AND THE MYTHS GO ON . . .

I f you have read this far, perhaps you are convinced that it is a good thing to question the things you believe. If you do so with a sincere heart toward God and integrity toward your fellow man, you will discover truths that will hold you in good stead both now and in the future.

Truth doesn't change. It is not twisted by tradition or someone's ideas or by organizational rules. Truth is truth and it *will* set you free. You can know you have taken hold of the truth by the freedom you experience: freedom from life-controlling sin, freedom from life-defining fear, freedom from guilt and shame, freedom to fulfill the plans that God has for you, freedom to love and be loved, freedom to do the right thing without regretting the cost. Truth is a wonderful thing that opens doors to abundance in life.

You can give yourself a checkup to see how you are doing with the truth.

- Do you respect others and have a healthy regard for yourself?

- Do you take responsibility for what you say and do?

- Do you have a tenacious devotion to understanding the Word of God for yourself?

- Do you leave room for the Holy Spirit to lead you into all truth, to bring to your mind the things you need to know, and to comfort you?

- Do you love the Lord?

- Do you allow your relationship with Him to be the preeminent relationship in your life?

- Is your relationship with Him more significant than your family of origin, your immediate family, your friends, and your work family?

- Is your relationship with Him more important than success, fame, or any fortune you might acquire?

- Do you minister to other people in Jesus' name?

If so, then you know freedom. None of us lives like this every moment, but as we mature, living free in Jesus becomes a more habitual manifestation of truth. For, you see, you have to come to the place where you have nothing to prove and nothing to lose. That is the life of a person who has found a life based in truth.

Our flesh loves to hold on to rights and loves to prove that *it* is right! You have heard these words before, but maybe in this context, you can see how relevant they are:

> *I have been crucified with Christ; and it is no longer I who live, but Christ lives in me; and the life which I now live in the flesh I live by faith in the Son of God, who loved me and gave Himself up for me.* (GALATIANS 2: 20)

If you have been crucified, you don't have anything to prove. You are dead. You don't have anything to lose. You have already lost it. So now that you live, it is Christ living through you. He isn't intimidated by the opinions of others, He isn't bound by the traditions of men, and He isn't needy of approval. He knows who He is and what He is about, and He walks in truth because He *is* the truth.

The freedom that pours forth from this empowering relationship with Christ, who is truth, can't be described. It can't be bought with a code of behavior. It is an understanding that allows you to live on a higher plane. You are not removed from life, but neither are you captive to what people think, or to their religious laws, or to their interpretations of truth. You are dead to those things, but you have a life in you—and it is Christ. If others know truth and walk in truth, you will find a oneness with them. It is in knowing, loving, and living the truth that we find a genuine bond of love and acceptance. There can and will be issues on which you will disagree, but they will not put you at war with one another. Like Paul and Barnabas, who disagreed over what to do about John Mark, you may go in separate directions (see Acts 15:39). That is fine, but that is not war. It is Satan, the old mythmaker himself, who tries to bring God's children into skirmishes that destroy the unity.

Myths keep you believing that you have to have people, position, or power to have contentment and peace. In one form or another, it is Satan's desire to keep you believing that original myth, *God is holding out on you, and God doesn't mean what He says.* In other words, the myth is that God is not enough for you and for your needs. If you take a look at the things that really matter to you in this life, no doubt each one can be altered or taken away from you. It is only your relationship with Christ—your love relationship with Him—that is good today and tomorrow and on into eternity.

THE HOLY SPIRIT

This relationship cannot be altered by the losses of life, the struggles of old age, or death. It transcends all of that. It is the love of Christ and your love for Him that is sustained through it all. And the wonderful part about that is that *He* is the sustainer. He is the one who is the same always and who never will leave. We are the ones who are weak and dim-sighted, but He loves us anyway and aims to get us home safely. That is why He said these words:

"But I tell you the truth, it is to your advantage that I go away; for if I do not go away, the Helper will not come to you; but if I go, I will send Him to you. And He, when He comes, will convict the world concerning sin and righteousness and judgment; concerning sin, because they do not believe in Me; and concerning righteousness, because I go to the Father and you no longer see Me; and concerning judgment, because the ruler of this world has been judged.

"I have many more things to say to you, but you cannot bear them now. But when He, the Spirit of truth, comes, He will guide you into all the truth; for He will not speak on His own initiative, but whatever He hears, He will speak; and He will disclose to you what is to come. He will glorify Me, for He will take of Mine and will disclose it to you. All things that the Father has are Mine; therefore I said that He takes of Mine and will disclose it to you." (JOHN 16:7–15)

When Jesus left us here on earth, He knew that we would need help. Since He was leaving, He had to send us someone to come alongside and get us through. Obviously, Jesus knew we needed to have a Helper, Counselor, and Guide, but wouldn't you know that the Enemy would have to swish his tail and mar that relationship as well?

One of the myths that has been perpetrated by the Enemy is the negation of the Holy Spirit. Oh, we know He is there, but we don't like to acknowledge Him too much. We don't want to be weird, and we often make fun of what we perceive to be His actions. But if you really consider how precious this longsuffering, third member of the Trinity is, it might change your view of the One who lives in you and shadows your every thought and move. He is not obtrusive, nor is He assertive.

He is faithful. He came when the Son went away. He is emotional—we know that He can be grieved (Ephesians 4:30). He is the source of your love, joy, peace, patience, and longsuffering (Galatians 5:22). He is your energy for service and your insight into the things of God (1 Corinthians 2:4). He is your antenna that goes up when things are said or done that aren't true or right. He is confirmation that what you have read, thought, or heard is indeed the truth of God (John 14:26).

It is His job to speak of the Lord Jesus Christ—He doesn't want the spotlight on Himself. He has never spotlighted Himself, but the Enemy has deceived us by putting a garish light on Him that almost makes us afraid to acknowledge that He is working.

If we believe what God tells us in the Scriptures about the person and work of the Spirit, then we won't be afraid of the still, small voice within that prompts us toward obedience, encourages us toward kindness, and convicts us when we have said something unkind. If we really want to honor His presence, we won't harden our hearts by withholding the love that He inspires us to give. We will dare to believe that it is only through love that others will know that we are followers of Christ. The Holy Spirit is the life-giver to you and to me. All that God does for us, He does through the Holy Spirit. Thank God that He remains with us until we are at home with Him. Take comfort from that and refuse the innuendoes of the Enemy. We have not been abandoned. You are not alone. He is here. God never has held out on us . . . He always has meant what He said. The Son came to save us and set us free. The Holy Spirit is here to bring us into all truth, to remind us of what Jesus told us, to convict us of sin, and to empower us for living the Christian life and ministry.

THE NO-HOPE MYTH

Satan loves it when we believe that we have messed up so badly that there is no hope. He loves to toss around the no-hope myth. He points to circumstances and laughs. He taunts us with, "You have made such a mess now, you might as well die." Ever been there?

He loves to convince us that what we have done has negated the promises of God. Or, he whispers the "awfuls" in our ear. "This is the most awful thing that could happen." The no-hope myth hangs around like a bad smell, waiting to attach itself to life's circumstances. He likes to slam the book shut and say, "That's it. You don't have a life!" Then God gently opens the book again and says, "The last chapter hasn't been written yet."

I saw my friends who lost two precious sons banish the no-hope myth and face life with the optimism of those who still have chapters to be written. They had a choice. They had grieved for years. They could continue retreating to their house while grieving their lives away, or they could grab the hope that God had promised and allow Him to continue to write a vibrant life story for them. That is your choice and mine. We can believe the no-hope myth, or we can believe God.

LOVE FOR GOD AND THE LOVE OF GOD

Life can be perplexing. We don't pick our platform and we don't pick our pain, but we can have hope even when things are so very dark. It isn't hope in changed circumstances because often they don't change. It is hope in God who "causes all things to work together for good to *those who love God"* (Romans 8:28, italics added). That is the key. He is active in the lives of those who love Him. A full-blown love for God is where you see things happen. I think we assume that because God loves us, He's got everything under control and that it doesn't really matter how we feel about Him as long as He is our Savior. Yet if you look at the Scriptures, you will see that He is very partial and highly involved with the one who loves Him.

> *"I, the LORD your God, am a jealous God, visiting the iniquity of the fathers on the children, on the third and the fourth generations of those who hate Me, but showing lovingkindness to thousands, to those who love Me and keep My commandments."* (EXODUS 20:5–6)

> *O love the LORD, all you His godly ones!*
> *The LORD preserves the faithful*
> *And fully recompenses the proud doer.*
> *Be strong and let your heart take courage,*
> *All you who hope in the LORD.*
>
> —PSALM 31:23–24

That is where our hope lives. It is in our passionate love relationship with Him.

> *And not only this, but we also exult in our tribulations, knowing that tribulation brings about perseverance; and perseverance, proven character;*

and proven character, hope; and hope does not disappoint, because the love of God has been poured out within our hearts through the Holy Spirit who was given to us. (ROMANS 5:3–5)

---- ✢ ----

THE HIGHEST AND BEST

"To be loved by God is the highest relationship, the highest achievement, and the highest position in life."

—*Henry Blackaby*

---- ✢ ----

HOPE

When you love God and know that you are loved by Him, you see the truth that permeates all the events of your life. He somehow lets you know that there is a bigger picture going on than you could ever imagine. The big things, the small things, the hard things, and the easy things are all shades of the big picture that He is creating of your life. Because He is the Creator and because He is the One who will write the last chapter, you can cling to a hope that will never disappoint.

Do you think for one moment that we will get to heaven, see our biography stretched out in front of us, and be disappointed at how it all came out? That's not our God. Although there may be some dark, hard chapters, by the time the last chapter is written we will be more and more in love with the Author. Satan hates that, so he constantly jumps in front of us and waves grim pictures of our circumstances in our faces, hoping to defeat us with despair. "Hopeless" is his whining cry.

"Hope is my gift to those who love Me" is God's response.

As long as you believe that there is hope, you can go on. As sisters in Christ, it is our duty to remind one another that there is hope. I believe that we can always encourage one another to find hope because we know God is at work behind the scenes, causing things to work for good—and that is a grand reason to love Him even more. No pain is wasted, no tragedy is trashed. He promises that our love for Him is the glorious motivation for Him to move heaven and earth to bring good out of our very hard and sad situations. And, of course, what is even more wonderful is that we love Him because He first loved us (see 1 John 4:19). There is no way to escape His love . . . and that gives us hope.

VICTIM

Myths are all around us. They are comfortable in their familiarity. They may be as simple as children's rhymes:

If you lie, your nose will grow.
If you step on a crack, you will break your mother's back.
If you cross your eyes, they will get stuck that way.

Those are the easy myths to spot. The hard ones involve our emotions and the beliefs that hit us in the deepest part of our souls.

I see many women who have been pulled into a murky side room of the Enemy and tattooed with a word they find hard to escape—*victim*. When life gets tough and hard things happen, Satan has a way of telling us that we are victims. That is a myth. We may have been victimized, but that in no way makes us a victim unless we chose to adopt that as our identity.

I believe this is one of the most delicate areas that we as women face in our truth-telling. A feeling of being powerless in the face of overwhelming odds leaves you feeling like a victim—and yet, hear me well, it is the feeling, not the circumstance that has you trapped.

The minute you see yourself as a victim, the door to freedom slams shut. A victim has no choices, and therefore no freedom. The truth is that the circumstances of your life do not define who you are. Your view of those circumstances defines you. Remember we have talked about the myth of everything is as it seems?

I have been talking with a dear, godly woman who has fallen into some very difficult circumstances. She began to see herself as a victim without choices, and she silently bore the pain. She sank deeper into a well of despair. Now she has her face against a wall and is trying to find just one place where she can get enough grip to climb out. I believe she will find her way up and over that huge wall of circumstance, but it isn't going to happen until she refuses to see herself as a victim and begins to see herself as a victor.

In Christ, you have options. Satan suggested to Eve that God had only one way for her to know life-fulfillment and that was to know good and evil. He also advanced the notion that God was holding out on her.

Eve saw herself as a victim of God's selfishness. "He's holding out on me. He doesn't mean what He says." Never mind that He had given her options. Every tree in the garden was available to her, but she took Satan's bait and zeroed in on the one tree God had forbidden. Eve acted like a victim.

The victim mentality is hard to crack. Because of the core belief "I have to look out for myself," it is difficult for women who see themselves as victims to open themselves to the healing power of the truth. If you want to experience truth, I would say to you, my sister, quit saying, " I am a victim of . . ." Challenge your thinking. "Where is it written" is a good place to begin. You may have been victimized, but you are not a victim. You may have been wounded, but you are not a wound. The focus is all wrong, and the myth is stifling.

If you want to breathe free air and take on a new identity, it is time to see the truth about yourself, life, and God. You are not a victim. You are a victor.

THE KINGDOM OF LIGHT

When you give your life to the Lord Jesus Christ, He takes up residence within you in the person of the Holy Spirit. That is the point where you are transferred from the domain of darkness into the kingdom of light.

> *For He rescued us from the domain of darkness, and transferred us to the kingdom of His beloved Son, in whom we have redemption, the forgiveness of sins.* (COLOSSIANS 1:13–14)

*You were formerly darkness, but now you are Light in the Lord; walk as chil-
dren of Light (for the fruit of the Light consists in all goodness and righteousness
and truth), trying to learn what is pleasing to the Lord.* (EPHESIANS 5:8–10)

Residents of the kingdom of light are not victims.

In her book *Invitation to Healing*, Lynda Elliott, who is a friend
of mine and a counselor, gives this illustration of a person who refused to let go of her victim mentality.

> An attractive woman named Cathy sat across the room from me,
> gripping the arms of the chair. As she told her story, her mouth was tight,
> her face drawn as she related her story. She said, "I was just denied a raise!
> My supervisor told me that my job performance was poor. I've never been
> good at anything. Every time I try something new, I hear my mother's
> voice reminding me how stupid I am! I fail at everything. I'll *never* be suc-
> cessful."
>
> As we continued to talk, it became evident that Cathy's mother had
> abused her. It also became evident that Cathy was making very little ef-
> fort to succeed. She had a record of poor work attendance, she failed to
> meet deadlines and she had an uncooperative attitude.
>
> When I challenged Cathy with these facts. She replied, "Well, I know
> that, but you see, if I ever really did become successful, my mother would
> feel absolved of the guilt for the abuse. She would believe that she hadn't
> really harmed me after all."
>
> Because Cathy had invested her life into proving that she was a vic-
> tim of childhood abuse, she had become totally enmeshed in her de-
> pression. Her life had not been invested in success. Instead, it had been
> an investment in bitterness, revenge and the desire for satisfaction.
>
> As Cathy struggled with the decision to change, she cried, "But, if I
> change now, I will have wasted 30 years! And my mother will never have
> to admit that she abused me . . ."
>
> While Cathy was living her life against her mother, she was also liv-
> ing it against herself.[1]

For the Christian, maintaining a victim identity distorts the truth.
In contrast, "If the Son makes you free, you will be free indeed" (John
8:36). You are free of the victim identity. It is now your privilege to

identify yourself as a victor. You can work out the issues of your victimization without maintaining a victim's mentality and identity.

THE FREEDOM OF TRUTH

As we come to the last page of *Moving Beyond the Myths,* I want to bring you back to the reason for this book. It was written so that you might be able to experience a freedom known only to a woman who knows the truth. We have pulled out many myths and placed them on the table for your examination. You may or may not agree with what I have identified as a myth. That is not the point. The point is to encourage you to ask yourself the question, "Where is it written?"

I have a passionate desire that women learn to think. If you will challenge yourself to look—and *keep* looking—God will meet you, and you will discover truth for yourself. If we achieve that goal, then our journey together has been successful. More than anything else, I want you to see Christ as you remove the myths. He is the One who makes truth a reality in our lives.

The following poems are by unknown authors. They paint a picture of the matchless One who is too precious to comprehend. He is the Truth Teller and the Truth Giver. He cuts through the myths with a sweet clarity that makes life complete.

-IN CHRIST WE HAVE:-

A love that can never be fathomed
A life that can never die
A righteousness that can never be tarnished
A peace that can never be understood
A rest that can never be disturbed
A joy that can never be diminished
A hope that can never be disappointed
A glory that can never be clouded
A light that can never be darkened
A purity that can never be defiled

A beauty that can never be marred
A wisdom that can never be baffled
Resources that can never be exhausted.

- CHRIST FOR ALL -

Christ for sickness, Christ for health,
Christ for poverty, Christ for wealth,
Christ for joy, Christ for sorrow,
Christ today and Christ tomorrow;
Christ my Life, and Christ my Light,
Christ for morning, noon and night,
Christ when all around gives way
Christ my everlasting Stay;
Christ my Rest, and Christ my Food
Christ above my highest good,
Christ my Well-beloved Friend
Christ my Pleasure without end;
Christ my Savior, Christ my Lord
Christ my Portion, Christ my God,
Christ my Shepherd, I His sheep
Christ Himself my soul to keep;
Christ my Leader, Christ my Peace
Christ hath wrought my soul's release,
Christ my Righteousness divine
Christ for me, for He is mine;
Christ my Wisdom, Christ my Meat,
Christ restores my wandering feet,
Christ my Advocate and Priest
Christ who ne'er forgets the least;
Christ my Teacher, Christ my Guide,
Christ my Rock, in Christ I hide,
Christ the Ever-living Bread,
Christ His precious Blood hath shed;

Christ hath brought me nigh to God,
Christ the everlasting Word
Christ my Master, Christ my Head,
Christ who for my sins hath bled;
Christ my Glory, Christ my Crown,
Christ the Plant of great renown,
Christ my Comforter on high,
Christ my Hope, draws ever nigh.

May you become one of the great host of women who discover freedom beyond your dreams as you move beyond the myths and walk in the truth.

Someday, we will meet in the wonderful kingdom He has prepared for us. Then we will know as we are known. Then there will be no lies.

Then we will have moved beyond every myth, and we will meet Truth face-to-face.

NOTES

Chapter One: Miserable Myths

1. Dan B. Allender, *The Healing Path: How the Hurts of Your Past Can Lead You to a More Abundant Life* (Colorado Springs: WaterBrook, 1999), 84.
2. Ibid., 85.

Chapter Two: Myths in the Garden

1. Brent Curtis and John Eldredge, *The Sacred Romance* (Nashville: Thomas Nelson, 1997), 56–57.

Chapter Three: The Myth of Damaged Goods

1. "Women's History in America Presented by Women's International Center," article excerpted from *Compton's Interactive Encyclopedia,* © 1994, 1995, Compton's NewMedia. Accessed through the Women's International Center Web site (www.wic.org), via the search engine for that site.
2. Marie Chapian, *A Confident, Dynamic You* (Ann Arbor, Mich.: Servant, 1997), 105.
3. See the discussion, "The Women Who Followed Jesus," *The Word in Life Study Bible: New Testament Edition* (New King James) (Nashville: Thomas Nelson, 1993), 242.
4. Ibid.
5. "Mary the Reliable Witness," *The Word in Life Study Bible,* 243.
6. Ibid.
7. Ibid.

Chapter Four: The Myth of Responsibility

1. Ken Johnson and Robert Tamasy, *Reflections from the Flock: Images of the Christian Life* (Denver: Accent, 1989), 36–37, 43.
2. Hannah Whitall Smith, *The Christian's Secret of a Happy Life* (New York: Revell, 1952), 38–39.
3. Richard Carlson, *You Can Be Happy No Matter What* (Novato, Calif.: New World Library, 1997), 52–53.
4. Geoff Gorsuch, "Journey to Adelphos," *Discipleship Journal,* 1 March 1983 (Issue 14), 7.

Chapter Five: The Myth of Marriage Is the Answer

1. From the sermon by Craig Barnes, "Learning to Speak Multiculturally," given at National Presbyterian Church, Washington, D.C., October 3, 1999.

Chapter Six: The Myth of Happy Little Women

1. Marie Chapian, *A Confident, More Dynamic You* (Ann Arbor, Mich: Servant, 1997), 107.

Chapter Seven: The Myth of Divorce Is the End

1. "How Can a Christian Begin to Heal?" Web site www.brokencircle.com, search at "How Can I Heal?" Used by permission.

Chapter Eight: The Myth of Everything Is As It Seems

1. Phillip McGraw, *Life Strategies* (New York: Hyperion, 1999), 151.
2. William Backus, *Telling the Truth to Troubled People* (Minneapolis: Bethany House, 1985), 76–77.
3. A. T. Beck, *Cognitive Therapy and the Emotional Disorders* (New York: Harper & Row, 1967), quoted in Backus, *Telling the Truth to Troubled People,* 76.
4. Ibid.
5. Ibid.
6. Ibid.
7. Ibid., 76–77.
8. McGraw, *Life Strategies,* 163.

Chapter Nine: The Myth of It's Possible to Play with Fire and Not Be Burned

1. William Backus, *The Hidden Rift with God* (Minneapolis: Bethany House, 1990), 85.
2. Letty Cottin Pogrebin, *Among Friends* (New York: McGrawHill, 1987), 81.
3. Gary Inrig, *Quality Friendship: The Risks and Rewards* (Chicago: Moody, 1981), 55.
4. Lori Thorkelson Rentzel, *Emotional Dependency* (Downers Grove, Ill.: InterVarsity, 1984, 1987, 1990; originally published in 1984 by Exodus International, San Rafael, Calif.), 15–16.
5. LeRoy Eims, *Be the Leader You Were Meant to Be* (Wheaton, Ill.: Victor, 1975), 105.

Chapter Ten: The Myth of Love

1. Ed Wheat, M.D., *Love Life for Every Married Couple* (Grand Rapids: Zondervan, 1980), 119–20.
2. Eugene Peterson, *The Message* (Colorado Springs: NavPress, 1995).

Chapter Eleven: The Myth of Church Is Always a Safe Place

1. Adapted from Sarah Sumner, *Christian Management Report,* March/ April 2000.
2. "Americans Describe Their Ideal Church," Barna Research Online, 7 October 1998. Web site: http://www.barna.org. All rights reserved.
3. Ibid.

Chapter Twelve: And the Myths Go On . . .

1. Lynda Elliott, L.S.W., *Invitation to Healing* (Little Rock, Ark.: LDE, 1999), 32.